This book is dedicated to my father, Keith Brown, with love.

Dad, you are my hero!

# Acknowledgment

There have been many friends and family members who have been a source of inspiration on my journey. Out of all of those, the main people I am extremely grateful for are my father, mother, sister, partner, and my son. They have been there through thick and thin.

My father was a single parent who struggled with multiple things in his life, from managing his own business to raising my sister and me while providing a roof over our heads. He also dealt with my recovery from the disease I was afflicted with, leading to surgery after surgery, hospital appointments, and after-effects. No parent likes to see their child in pain, and all they can do is watch with guilt and think, “Why is this happening to my child?”

Even though he supported my needs for eighteen years and stayed strong for me, he always succeeded in hiding his sadness. Although sometimes he does not agree with my decisions, he always stands by my side and supports me.

I remember the time my father drove to pick me and my sister up from our mother’s place. When we arrived outside our house, my father told us to be quiet. We both were unsure why. When our father opened the door, I saw a kitten poking his head out from the living room corner. I had the biggest smile on my face. I begged my father

# The Beautiful Survivor

The Beauty Within Our Struggles

Kaylie Louise

ISBN: 978-1-959392-41-5

to get a cat, and he always refused. But that day, I came home to be with my family, and that's when our father told my sister and me that the kitten was a boy. He was a tabby and really tiny. My father asked me what to name him. I called him *'Tommy,'* from the famous cartoon, *'Tom and Jerry.'* To this very day, Jason and I have our own cat, which we bought when we began living together.

When I moved away from home, I decided that my cat, Tommy, should stay with my father. It was his home, and I did not want to take him away from his home, and my father did love him. When Tommy passed away, I wanted to carry on his name. I tried to find a cat who was a tabby and of the male sex. But the cat Jason and I found was a female cat and needed a home. So, we named her Tia to carry out the letter 'T' from my cat, Tommy.

I could not have asked for a better father. I look up to him and try to follow in his footsteps.

I have one sister, someone who is three years younger than me. We have both been through tough times in the past. However, we are still very close today. We are closer today than we have been in the past.

We used to play in our childhood. However, when she reached school and made her own friends, we drifted apart as we did not have time for each other. As they say, things change when people get older.

When we both hit our teens, we loved going to *'Westfields Shopping Centre'* in Stratford together. We had our music playing loudly from the car, singing along, with our voices being loud and heard by the people we passed. We would always be laughing and enjoying. We would make funny faces along with the music because that's how we would interact with our silliness.

My sister wasn't a shopping person. She loved to shop in game stores and certain clothing stores. We both had our favourite shops we used to love when we were younger. We both loved the shop called *'Paperchase.'* We were into stationary, and I remember she loved the rubbers that looked like food or objects.

Even though we have our disagreements, I know she will always be by my side, no matter what. That's what sisters are for.

When it comes to my partner, he inspired me by being the man I truly deserve, the man I need in my life. He showed his real self to me and treated me the way I should be treated.

After the tragedy with my ex, my current partner opened my eyes to a new world, where I found a new beginning. He never stops me from achieving my dreams. I found a listener in him. He always puts all his energy into fixing certain situations. He also always protects my mental health and has never made me feel worthless.

The last two years we have spent together have been

amazing, and we have decided to get married later this year. I also went through IVF and was blessed with our perfect baby boy, Daniel. I know my partner loves me wholeheartedly because he went through all these adversities with me. I do not think I would have found him if I did not search for him.

Everything I have gone through, the good and the bad, has made me the person I am today. I have discovered how beautiful it is to follow your heart, but my growth as an individual has not ended yet. I am still growing and finding out what I want in life. You only live once, so you may as well make it worth it, right?

My son Daniel was born on the 31st of January, 2022. He is my everything.

The one who I want to give everything to. I want to see him grow up into an amazing person and help others. I hope I can give him what he deserves and appreciate what he has.

Going through IVF to have him wasn't short of a miracle. He is a miracle. It feels like he's the one. He's the one who stayed in my tummy because he knew how much I wanted him.

I give him all my love, and I will never let him go. I'll give him my strength, honesty, love, and protection. He knows I will be the best mother I can be, and I will always adore him with all my heart.

# Contents

# About the Author

When it comes to writing about myself, I believe I can go on forever and ever. There is so much that needs to be noted, and I want everyone to know the real me. People usually form various assumptions about us throughout our lives, and I can ensure they have judged me and have supposed that I am leading a simple life. Mainly because from the outlook, everything seems normal. But they have never walked in my shoes. People get surprised and cannot believe their ears when I tell them about my struggles.

I consider myself a girly girl fond of shopping, make-up, and, obviously, bags. However, I am also interested in games, driving, and action movies. So yes, I am basically a mixture of everything. From the description I have given you, I may come across as a happy-go-lucky person who has only faced a few problems in her life. But that is not the case.

My parents separated when I was just a mere child. I vividly recall how I suffered from Meningitis and Septicemia, which was a horrible time. It is true that I have gone through many hardships. But when I reached the age of twenty-five, all these diseases held their horses eventually.

Whenever I thought about executing my dreams, my surgeries would come in the way and cause my mental state and physical appearance to go downhill. I always found a way to bring myself back up again, but it was never easy. There are so many dreams I want to accomplish, and I know one by one, I will achieve them all.

At such a young age, I desired to be loved by someone. To take the pressure off my father and someone to take the responsibility to love and care for me. Love is my main goal. Love is a mixture of different factors. My definition of love is to be happily married to my husband and have an amazing family. For others, it may vary, such as traveling the world or having a successful career. People can have different definitions of love and be happy anyways.

Every journey appears to be a roller-coaster ride, but you must be strong enough to hold on tight, no matter how difficult it is. Your dreams will and can only come true if you keep fighting and encourage yourself never to give up. I have been told by people that I'm a fighter. But I don't think I am, even though it is the truth. It's because there was no other choice, life threw different things at me, and I HAD to get through them all.

I was born in London, UK, and now reside in Essex. I love the views of living in the countryside and London is not suitable for me. I find the atmosphere too crowded and suffocating to breathe in.

When it was time for me to move out of my father's place and start my journey into the real world, I decided to do so. I did not want to leave, but I knew I must go and live my life someday.

Singing would be my main profession, but if only I could sing! But honestly, I don't have the voice to appear on the X-Factor. I was clueless about what occupation would be the best for me until college. I finally realised that I wanted to become a Magazine Designer. It involves a variety of artwork, and where there is art, there is me.

My inspiration to become a Magazine Designer was from the film '*13 Going on 30.*' I thought it would be perfect for me. I proceeded to attain my qualifications in college but happened to find out I would need to go to university. I did not have the courage to go. No part of me wanted to leave home and put myself in a situation where I had to worry about finances. I had other dreams, which meant much more to follow and reach.

When I was a child, I used to love writing stories. I used to draw the characters from the cartoon 'Powerpuff Girls.' My favourite was 'Bubbles,' and my sister loved 'Blossom.' We used to sit together at my father's table and create stories together.

When I reached my teens, my diary had become my best friend. I penned down everything that came to my mind. I am still writing to this day and hope my story will get published in the future.

My mother knew my sister and I have loved art ever since we were young girls. She made her living room into our bedroom. She created the room with art items, and our desks were stretched across the room. We had everything you can think of.

I hope readers who read my story acknowledge they are not alone. I hope they find the courage to follow their hearts and dreams. Everybody goes through different struggles, but how we become stronger despite all the adversities is what matters.

There may be moments you will feel alone and need to remember to be grateful for what you have. Always be thankful because your life is better than it could be. Some people can help you throughout your troubles. Family, friends, and even people who you may not know. There is always someone.

Only you can turn your life around and make it better. People around you can only do what they can do. You need to be the person to keep fighting and believe in yourself. You only live once, and I hope my book will help you find your way in life and be happy.

# Preface

There are two types of people in the world. The ones who get everything they desire in life without making any effort. Then there are those who struggle day and night, waiting for a miracle to happen to them, so their dark lives are brightened.

I consider myself the second one. As the name suggests, this book, The Beautiful Survivor, is about me, a strong woman who dealt with every adversity that life threw her way with immense strength. If it weren't for my sheer dedication and hard work to achieve what I wanted, things would not be the same as they are today.

So much had gone wrong in my life. My parents' separation, a weighty decline in my well-being, breaking up with a significant other, and not being able to conceive like other women. Despite all these difficulties, I never chose to give up and kept fighting like a warrior.

This written work reflects my struggles and how I managed to get through them. I also aim to spread my message and motivate those who have gone through a broken relationship. I know how my ex-fiancé impacted my mental health, but I never gave up on love (you shouldn't either).

I still embarked on the journey to find true love. And you know what they say. Whatever you wish for eventually comes to you if you set your heart to find it. I found a man who truly loves me and stood by my side during the painful process of IVF. And the gift of our patience came in the shape of our beautiful baby boy named Daniel.

I hope that this book proves to be a source of inspiration for those who need it most. And I sincerely wish that you never give up on your dreams because your share of happiness is present in the world; you just have to be courageous enough to find it.

# Chapter 1
# The Purpose of My Story

*"The pain can feel devastating, and all you want is for the pain to diminish or for someone else to heal your wounds. Always look over your loved ones, and protect them from pain and misery. By not letting them suffer, show them that you're stronger than anything else."*

*– Kaylie Louise*

Sharing your personal life with the world or people you haven't met before is like stripping your garments off. You have to remove each piece of cloth covering your wounds, your miseries, your struggles and your efforts to overcome them, your achievements, victories, and the little and big moments of happiness in your life. It is indeed an act of sheer courage and bravery to carry all those pieces of yourself and the remnants of your past into a future where you can construct a renewed life without looking back at anything at all.

However, the process of shedding is rather easier than evolving into the same skin. I'm not sure if my desire to share my story with you is going to serve a utilitarian purpose or not, but I am sure that my intention is to uplift those who have been on a similar path as mine, and I am hoping it would be able to do that at least.

Of course, every individual has a different take on life. Some people live and feed on their past experiences because it helps them grow into successful beings. Others choose to completely eradicate their memories because it obstructs their growth as a person and prevents them from being sane, let alone being successful. In my case, I think it is an amalgamation of both lenses that helped me progress into the individual that I am today. In fact, it is always the struggle between choosing to give up and succumbing to the crises and, on the other hand, striving to set foot beyond the crises in the hope of a better future. Our struggle between these two and subsequently our final decision determines our present and alters aspects of our personality in the process.

This world is not a safe place to live in; it is scary, it is unpredictable, and for the greater part, it is tremendously complicated. We wake up, each day unknown, unaware of the path we will tread upon on that particular day. We spend it in complete darkness of what lies ahead of us even after we've managed to get through those 24 hours. No matter how many fortune-tellers or astrologists we end up interacting with, there's no supernatural force of precognition that can tell us what lies ahead; we are still humans at the end of the day. Going through a journey of struggles that inflicts pain upon you and your loved ones is a part of your life, and so is the ability to cope with losses and act normally after grieving. Even though something like that should not be normalised, unfortunately, it has been the case for centuries.

If there is one thing I learnt that has remained true through the ages is the fact that *life does not stop for anyone at all.* Regardless of the internal pain or external wounds you bear, the demise of a loved one that breaks you apart, the loss of a roof over your head because of financial crises that have left your family stranded, or the simplest heartbreak of someone not loving you back, no matter how harsh your life is with you, it is expected that you will cope. Even though it is a bitter reality, believe it or not, it is the only way to survive this life and eventually find your destined way in this world.

My purpose in putting you on that emotional rollercoaster was not to take away your light but rather to show you in all its transparency that this is how it is. You are not alone in your struggles; it is important for you to know and feel other people's pain and struggle and identify both the similarities and differences between others with your life. It is essential that you go through this process because it will help you appreciate your own struggles by knowing that there are worse things that influence people's lives; there are some individuals who go through cascades of catastrophes, one after the other, and life refuses to take it easy on them.

In all honesty, I would say I am one of those people that you'll be interacting with through this book. I am a person defined by dreams that were lost and found, pain borne, which eventually diminished castles built on hope and relentless skirmishes that made me stronger throughout my life. Even today, I may not predict what will happen tomorrow because my destiny is not in my hands. However, I know that whatever I have to face, I will do so with all the courage and strength I have in my soul, and I will make sure I do not fail without even trying my best. Trying is a significant measure of your valour and your evolved capacity for survival.

We are all an outcome of our experiences in life; the good, bad, the worst, and the best. As a consequence of our cumulative encounters, we become stronger and tougher to thrive in this world, which is a maze of unpredicted troubles and blessings. Once we do that, voila, we know we have learnt the tactic of not giving up.

However, when you barely understand why you are faced with such trials, the journey to get your life together and handling everything that comes your way in a much decent manner is not easy at all. It comes with pain and with a constant urge of wanting to surrender to your circumstances. Therefore, you need to make a conscious effort to recognise your patterns of approach to your problems and identify what you need to change in them.

It is in motivational speakers, quotations, internet videos, and social media where most of us tend to find comfort. The reason being that the people who pen down those quotes or write those video scripts and eventually gather the strength to share their experiences with you have also been through the same process of endurance. It is because you and those people had something mutual to connect with; the disguised or explicit messages in those videos and write-ups resonate with you. Anything that your eyes fall upon and your ears remain hooked on is surely being processed in your mind and eventually stored in your conscious, subconscious, and unconscious thoughts.

When you read or hear things, you naturally sift among them. The ones that are relevant to your current motive remain in your conscious thoughts. On the other hand, those things that strike you somewhere in your system tend to slide down into your subconscious. Still, those would only come to the surface when you eventually encounter a relevant situation where that thought plays itself like a recorded reel. Lastly, there are a lot of things that we choose to consider unnecessary or count as irrelevant in our lives.

Apparently, nothing is ever unnecessary. Everybody goes through various processes in life at different stages; nobody has a set or defined time of experiencing things or feelings such as trauma, failure, or even pride. Therefore, there are a lot of things that we unconsciously allow to slide past our conscious level of understanding. At the same time, there is also a possibility that people around you make you feel that those things are unimportant and you shouldn't pay much attention. Hence, you repress those feelings and problems. However, what you unconsciously do is build a pile of unconscious thoughts that eventually come to haunt you or remind you of their importance and presence in your life in the form of a dream.

Dreams are not always the best thing to deal with. Sometimes, our dreams overwhelm our existence in the present and prevent us from moving forward more than our conscious thoughts and actions do. In those circumstances, some meditation and some time away from those dreams and thoughts are necessary. It is important to divert your mind to something that you can connect with instead of feeling lost and miserable on your journey to an unknown path in life.

Like I said before, I want to affirm again that you are not alone in your struggles. You are not the only one who thinks that life is not taking it easy on you, and you certainly aren't the only one who is pessimistic about life. We all are, or at least a majority of the world is, and those who aren't have found a way to divert their negativity into optimistic thoughts.

Just as those social media quotes and videos resonate with you, I also hope that my book and experiences will resonate with you. Even if my experience itself does not help you connect, I am sure that the underlying message will. The uncontrollable cascade of trauma, along with a natural vulnerability to give up, but eventually pushing myself to seek the strength to keep going amidst all those experiences - I am sure each one of you has gone through a similar process. Yet I am certain that all those reading this have or are finding the motivation to cope, survive, and eventually come out grateful at the end, with or without the support of those around you.

I am as transparent, brutally honest, and just as anxious as anyone would be to share their life with others. However, I am convinced that the world will become a better place for us with shared experiences, and I intend to do just that. I want you all to remain strong, constant, and supportive of my journey by continuing to flip the pages of my life in this book and so allowing it to settle in your mind as a keepsake; a keepsake to remind you that you will not give up, no matter what happens. I have no words about how I am still standing here today, but I know that you must keep going as I did and look where it brought me. You and I have a few or maybe more things in common, and in order to find our mutual ground, you have to take a leap of faith and trust me on this journey. Let's start!

# Chapter 2
# Tracing Back to the Beginning

My parents were unmarried, yet they chose to bring my sister and me into this world. I'm genuinely grateful to my parents for bestowing life upon me. However, I have a serious grievance that I intend to bring to the surface. There are some things that parents often don't pay attention to while raising their children; it's their emotional and mental well-being.

Parents rarely pay heed to their children's psychological growth. How the world influences their offspring and how their children develop certain fears and inabilities to tackle real-life challenges, they stay indifferent to these matters. This is due to their own shortcomings and marital clashes, especially as children do not speak for themselves. One such traumatic rollercoaster that I once had to ride on was the split between my parents. As a child, it was difficult for me to comprehend the whole concept of my parents' willingly opting for separation, knowing that it would cause an emotional and mental troubling rift in my sister's and my life.

I was barely seven years old when my parents separated. For some reason, that moment remains vividly outlined in my memory forever, inflicting the same amount of pain, misery, and grief that I had experienced at the moment itself. But at the same time, I felt relieved that they had separated. I saw they had good times. But after some time, they were not happy throughout the time when they were together. I believe my mother used her maternal right to take me with her, and my consent did not matter at that age. Even though I badly wanted to be with my father, I did not have a choice in the matter.

I was really upset about moving away from him. I wasn't happy about my mother's decision to move in with her boyfriend at his place. I honestly did not like that man at all; I believe he was an alcoholic, and living in his house did not add to my mental stability. It further deteriorated it. I lived under the same roof with my mother and her boyfriend while watching their episodes of physical violence and shouting. I knew it was not a healthy environment, and yet, I could do nothing while my mother cried for hours near the door. There were times where he always seemed to walk out the door and go down to the pub. In fact, when I thought about domestic violence, I was not prepared to view it at all.

When my mother was moving out, she naturally expected me to move along with her boyfriend and herself to his place. There was no effort made to ask or discuss what I wanted from my life. No one asked me if I wanted to stay with her, whether I was emotionally and physically ready to leave the house where we had been living previously or to drift away from my father.

Nobody bothered to try and find out, and they clearly did not want to know; they didn't care less. It was a difficult time and situation. The family was falling apart. There was no time to figure out the best solution for my sister and me. My parent's relationship ended badly. I had no idea what my father was going through as I wasn't with him. It was heartbreaking. But I knew my parents were better off separated. I was already out of place living with my mother and her boyfriend. Every day, each moment in time, all I wished for was to meet my father somehow. I was really attached to him. I just needed a glance, a moment to share, a while to talk and connect with him; I just wished that my father was around.

As a child, I struggled with the one trait that most of you may have dealt with, and that was expressiveness. It was always so tough for me to express myself. I used to experience a burst of emotions on a daily basis, a surge of feelings altogether, and I wanted to say so much all at once; I at least wanted to yell or whine, but I never could. I have a sharp memory of this incident where my mother's boyfriend was once arguing with her, and he was drunk out of his mind. I think it was the first time in my life that I endured a mix of emotions altogether, and my inability to express them led to the worst kind of consequence of uncontrolled, untreated, and repressed emotions.

There was an intense amount of physical violence taking place in front of my eyes, and I found myself helpless. My mother's boyfriend was pushing her, shouting at her, and both were pulling each other. She was crying while clinging to the door. When these incidents would happen, she would feebly cry at the door. There was no other place of shelter that my mother had, so this was her only refuge, given that she couldn't go back to my father because their relationship was already over.

I was extremely disappointed at how my mother was being treated by her boyfriend, but more than that, I was unhappy because my father wasn't around to protect us and keep us safe. I wanted my father to see what was happening and how we were growing up affected by intense domestic violence. Out of my powerlessness, the only action that made sense to me was to divert my unsettled feelings by setting the bin on fire. It was as though the fire was quenching my rage, frustration, and grievances against my mother and her boyfriend.

I sat in front of it, and I continued to gaze at the fire I had ignited; I kept following the fluctuation of the flames as they rose and dropped. With my chaotic emotions, I could feel the inconsistency of the flame resonated and reminded me of my sense of emptiness, despite feeling the high tide of emotions racing within. In simple words, I was unhappy because I wanted my father to come around and take us out of that miserable place. Looking at the flame in the bin from the bathroom, I changed my mind and threw water from the sink to put it out. A small cloud of black smoke appeared, and I ran straight into my bedroom. My heart was pounding fast.

Soon after this incident, we happened to be driving through a street that was engulfed in darkness. My sister and I were tucked in the backseat while my mother was driving us around with her boyfriend in the passenger seat. She ended up parking outside a street, and even though I wasn't old enough to know the location, I clearly remember the place where she parked because it was right outside my school. I sort of knew or at least had an instinct of what was going on. Although, I wasn't completely sure.

Suddenly, without any warning, I saw my father in the street. He walked towards our car. I saw him from the rear-view mirror. My father walked up to my mother, they got into an argument, and I saw her crying incessantly after that. My father also got emotional. I could see both my parents fighting for us. Both wanted us to themselves. I remember my mother having all her belongings in the car. I knew this time my mother did not have anywhere to live. I believe that is why my father showed up. On the spur of the moment, my father opened the car's back door, and he asked my sister and me to come with him. He picked me up from the seat and held me in his arms while he held my sister by her hand, and we walked away from the car. He took us away from our mother while she cried helplessly.

All I saw of my mother while growing up was that she was alone and helpless, and that was more or less because she couldn't decide what to do and when to do it. I believe my mother knew she was with the wrong person but was unable to take the right actions.

She never had the motivation to take any action. The further we walked away from that day onward, we kept distancing from our mother, and she kept going further and further away. From that point on, we began to live with our father alone. We were still happy compared to our previous state of mind and physical discomfort too.

We did not quite understand what was happening with our mother; we weren't sure how we were with our mother just a few days before, and sometime after, we found ourselves back with our father, with no clue of our mother in the picture or otherwise. Back at that time, it made no sense to me what was happening and why. I felt and hoped that my mother would not continue the relationship with her boyfriend.

While living with my father, I remember that I was with my sister one night, and my father was watching TV in the lounge. I ambled downstairs and told him that I was finding it really hard to sleep. He poured me some water, handed me the glass, and told me to go back to sleep once I was done drinking, assuming it would soothe me and make me sleepy. However, I remained wide awake even after that glass of water.

It was on one of those nights when I couldn't sleep at all. Therefore, I went back to bed, and I continued sobbing and whimpering for fifteen minutes straight. I finally mustered the courage to walk down to my father that night. He was in the kitchen, and he immediately had me sit on the kitchen counter. Soon, I saw him melt something blue; he melted the blue dots and poured them over my arms and on my chest area.

As soon as he applied those melted dots on my body, he asked me to go into the room until he could call the ambulance. He was extremely calm with me and so placid about the whole situation. I am sure he was as paranoid as I felt inside with my condition, but he handled everything smoothly. When he asked me to go in, I agreed and quietly resorted to the room because I felt so weak. Within less than five minutes of my father's call, the ambulance arrived, and two men came in.

Those men from the ambulance looked at me, examined me, and said that I needed to be taken to the hospital and needed to be placed in the ambulance. They were gentle, and they carried me into the ambulance. I was lying down on a stretcher, as I remember, looking at my father and my sister while I saw life flashing in front of my eyes.

I had an oxygen mask fixed on my face and could only see half of the things beyond the mask. I was feeling terribly weak, as though I was drained of life. I was so sick, and it constantly felt like a heavyweight was suppressing and pushing my body, which prevented me from moving at all.

After the ambulance, I was rolled into a room full of doctors on the stretcher, from what I recall. I could only see my father and my sister standing behind a blue curtain, which segregated the operation or diagnosis area from the spectating arena. I felt like my life was being taken away from me because my body had no control over itself at that point.

While I struggled to stay put in that bed, unknown of my condition and the probabilities of losing or surviving, I suddenly saw my mother appear out of nowhere. I couldn't quite understand the cause, motivation, and means of her return. She appeared in front of my face, crying and holding my hand as if she would never let go. It was immediately after that when I began throwing up.

I was feeling awfully nauseous, and each time they tried putting the mask on my face, I ended up throwing up in the mask as well. While I was constantly throwing up without knowing how to stop vomiting and without having any control over how my body reacted at that point, my last vision of myself saw big, nasty needles all over my body. They had pierced many of them in my body, and the moment I realised that, I fell asleep or rather unconscious due to its toll on me. This is all I remember from that time when I was heavily sedated.

When I opened my eyes from that long sedation, I found myself in the hospital only. However, this time around, it wasn't the same room where I was initially taken. This room was colossal in its space; it looked and felt like a hotel room suite with its interiors and the amenities it contained and provided. The room I found myself in was different, and so was I. I did not feel as if I was the same child anymore; I felt nothing like before.

There were no remnants of myself from my past carried into this new, alienated and distinct self of mine. I felt different because I felt lost with no recollection of who I used to be. I actually felt like I knew nothing. It felt like I was washed, purified, or experiencing a complete eradication of who I was. It took me a while to awaken my senses, acclimatise with my surroundings and my new existence, and only when I finally gained complete consciousness was I told that I was in a coma for a few days. The number of days or time remained unknown, but it was clear that the sedation had done something that my existence wasn't prepared for.

During my stay at the hospital, I was taken for trips to the surgery room. It felt like I was going on a field trip daily. However, it wasn't all fun and games there. I found myself covered in bandages. I did not have much of an appetite, and I barely ate anything. I was heavily surviving on food and liquid drips; drips infused into my body kept me alive and not substantial food anymore. After a few weeks of coma and minor surgeries at the *St. Mary Paddington Hospital*, the surgeons handling my case decided to transfer me to the Burns Unit at the *Chelsea and Westminster Hospital*. I was admitted there for an extensive period of 6-9 months. Luckily, my mother was able to stay with me, while my father also had my sister to look after.

However, I was just existing and not living. I couldn't walk; I was shackled to my wheelchair. I underwent multiple surgeries to fix the nerve and muscle damage and the foot-drop abnormality my body collapsed under. I had a rickety body altogether, which couldn't stand its weight due to nerve and muscle damage within my body. The surgeries were conducted for years. Transporting and shifting me from one room to another due to surgeries. Certain surgeries needed me to be in a room to fight infections due to Meningitis Septicemia.

From my memories and flashbacks at the hospital, I remember feeling the scars that I have now, which were fresh back then; they were black, as though my skin was rotting. When the bandages were removed, everything was pitch black. My life seemed to have lost colour and vibrancy. All I saw were the surgery theatre lights, the hospital beds, bandages, and my black scars. There was no ray of hope amidst those hospital walls; it was all weary and weird. I honestly did not know what to make of everything that was happening to me. There was a thick ray of blurriness in front of my eyes and my existence.

Between my past and healthy self and between the present damaged self, I had to cross a thick blurred line to reach an unknown future awaiting my presence. I had also developed a hearing impairment, the impact of which made my hearing ability worse. With a body so fragile that I had to depend on others, and an inability to express myself, losing my sense of hearing, was nothing but a living nightmare. I was already struggling to connect or find hope in anything emotionally, and losing my senses along with blurred vision and little or no appetite, I felt more or less like a zombie without the ability to walk.

My scars – those burnt scars became permanent and failed to disappear no matter how hard the Burns Unit nurses and doctors tried to pale them out. It became a part of my identity, which certainly did not feel good. I remember being taken into a massive bathtub where they used to soak me; they would immerse me into the bathtub and have all the bandages pulled away from my skin. It was scary, terrifying, and blood-wrenching. The cycle repeated itself to pale out my stains so that they could put a special dressing on them.

What was worse was the fact that even though I was going through all those painful surgeries and the torturous bandaging sessions, I still had the scars on me at all times. I remember laying on my bed and observing my left hand, and then my whole body was more or less damned with blackness. It was a mark on my identity that refused to leave me alone. The emotional and physical turmoil that those scars had inflicted on me was indescribable, but in simple words, it was horrible.

# Chapter 3
# The Beauty Within Our Struggles

## Miracle

Apart from the pain that I endured from the constant surgeries, the burns, and the constant changing of bandages during my extended stay in the hospital, I had another worry that made me very anxious. My legs had no strength in them, and my arms would not support me after the havoc that *Meningitis Septicemia* wreaked on my body. I could not even sit in the wheelchair and had to be helped into it by the nurses.

Being confined to a wheelchair and unable to walk or run was debilitating and depressing. I thought I would never walk again. I was living my life in a wheelchair. I was losing hope. I thought my life would end like this.

But at such a low point in my life, when I thought it was all over and I would be eking out my days like this, dependent on others for care when something amazing and wonderful happened. I was finally considered well enough to start physiotherapy. It gave me a new lease on life, and I was finally able to take control of my wilting body.

My physiotherapy sessions were transformative for me. The physiotherapist worked hard to awaken my dormant muscles, and I started having hope again. It was not a quick process and took a really long time. But, as they say, *"no pain, no gain."* The physiotherapy exercises continued day after day, and I had to attend them, even when I had no strength and would just want to lie in bed and not move an inch.

I would turn my face to the wall, but the physiotherapist would not give up on me. The sweat used to roll off my face as the doctors pushed me to exert and push myself to the utmost limits. My legs would tremble with the movements, my muscles would ache, and I was so stiff that I could not even sit. But gradually, I started noticing a change as the wasted muscles of my body started strengthening.

I could still not walk, but I could feel a difference in my energy even though it was muted. I kept telling myself to be patient and keep striving towards my goal. I felt all I could do was just to continue following what I was told.

The interesting part is that I couldn't recall every physiotherapy session, but what I can recall now is that they were too many to count. I had to go through the therapy sessions every day except when the doctors said to skip the physiotherapy session because of the surgeries. The obvious reason for missing the therapy sessions was that I felt extremely weak and feeble after each of my surgery.

I also had physiotherapy sessions on the hospital bed when the therapist would walk into my room because I wasn't even able to move my body a bit. After a few sessions on the bed, I started visiting the therapy room in a wheelchair. Every time I visited that room, it fascinated me a lot because huge machines were installed inside and different types of equipment were in the room. I used to feel better in that room because the equipment there really attracted me as a child, and I would say that I just wanted to be away from the hospital room as much as I could somehow.

All this was happening, and my doctors and I were trying hard to make me recover quickly, but there were times when I used to cry. I had to push myself hard after going through the surgeries. I felt like I returned to where I started my therapy, no matter how hard I tried to improve. What added to worsening the situation was that I felt I was failing, and that feeling of being failed again and again despite trying was heart-shattering.

Yet, I sometimes also laughed and felt happy when my body showed even a little progress. Whenever the doctor said that my body was improving, the hope to get better soon strengthened in my heart; I wouldn't be able to describe those feelings ever. When nothing was working at all, even the slightest move to recover meant a lot.

My feet had no strength in them to walk even with help, so

I used to wear splits on both of my feet to keep them off the ground. Gradually I made myself comfortable with the splits, and one day when I thought I had to keep them with me forever, the therapist gave me a weirdly shaped frame. I had seen people using a crutch to aid them in walking, and I know that's absolutely normal. But I was provided with a frame. Perhaps it was because I wasn't able to hold the crutch with my left hand. At the start, I was sceptical about using the frame, but later on, it actually helped me a lot to start walking.

As the weeks passed by, my physiotherapist wanted me to try walking without the frame; he guided me to take smaller steps first. Then motivated and encouraged me to take small steps and move my feet. Even though I was progressing slowly and steadily, I had the biggest smile on my face because I hoped that I would be walking someday soon. It was my miracle, and I couldn't believe it. Even now, I find it hard to believe that I can walk on my own after the various episodes of such a serious illness.

The months passed by in a blur, and finally, that day arrived. It was when the miracle happened, and I got to walk again.

*"Hold yourself responsible for a higher standard than anybody else expects of you. Never excuse yourself. Never pity yourself. Be a hard master to yourself and be lenient to everybody else."*

-Henry Ward Beecher

This miracle that I was blessed with is one of the reasons why I am sharing my story of struggle with the world because I want my readers to understand that life is not a bed of roses; it is unfair, messy, and difficult.

*But then again, who has ever said that life is easy?*

It was so tough for me to push myself out of that wheelchair and learn to walk again. But, if you do not have hope, if you lack willpower and the resolve and determination to succeed, you will end up exactly where you started. You will be moving in circles, stuck in the same cycle, instead of carving your own path.

Another major problem that I suffered from my condition was memory loss. I was unaware of my memory loss disease phase until my parents told me; I got to know about it when I was in my teens. I could not remember things, and I forgot how to write and read. I had no memory of my studies and the things I was taught. Every day I struggled to remember what had happened the day before, only to be met with a blank slate. No matter how much I tried to write on it, it stayed blank. It brought back memories of my childhood when I was given the opportunity to adjust.

With the passage of time, I was able to recall flashbacks to a time when I couldn't recall anything. I remembered how well I knew my math schedules and how beautifully I used to write. People would say things to me that I didn't understand or had never heard before.

But as my body healed and started working again, so did my mind. Gradually, bits and pieces of my memory started popping in and leaving. As I began to relearn the things I had once known, my knowledge came back again. I could still not remember my past physical state, but I could recall certain past events. I was reborn, and I had been given a new life.

It was a disease, and I'm not sure I'll ever fully comprehend why it came to me. I became ill before I was able to receive my vaccines while children my age were receiving them. It has always been tough for me to adjust my capabilities, and it still is on occasion. It's strange how vividly I recall every minute of my illness. I seem to recall the things I want to remember as well as the awful events I don't want to recall.

While I was in the hospital with little to do except lie in bed or go for surgeries and physiotherapy, I started feeling lost. Luckily, there were many activities that patients could participate in at the hospital. I started taking part in some of them, and the one I really enjoyed was being on the hospital radio. It was a brand new experience for me, and it turned out that it was something that I truly loved. It really brightened up my day and made me feel alive.

As years passed by, a club formed at the hospital for children who suffered burns. I was included in it due to my illness which physically resembled the burns they had. Children of different ages were included, and they participated in a campsite at 'Grafham Waters.' I met children all around the UK and around the world.

There was the staff who looked after us, and it felt like it was a holiday. I attended the event once a year without fail. It was an amazing experience for me. I did many activities I never thought I could and had so much fun. They organised bike riding, windsurfing, canoeing, rock climbing, disco parties, theme park events, sitting around campfires, and many more.

I stayed in the hospital for around six to nine months. I went through so much there during that time. I arrived in such a bad shape that my family was not sure whether I would pull through or not. They put me back together, at the hospital and I will always be grateful to them and their excellent care.

Despite all the painful treatments, I have some good memories of my hospital stay, and they make me smile today. The nurses were really nice to me. I remember a guy at the hospital who used to push my wheelchair really fast through the corridors and make me feel like we were racing down the corridors, running away from the misery and pain around us. It used to put a big smile on my face.

Another fascinating feature of my time at the hospital was being chosen by the radio department. Most people at the hospital knew who I was, and I had formed a relationship with them. My mother used to take me to the radio department in my wheelchair.

They pushed me to the opposite side of the department because I resided on the top floor.

Every time I was taken out of the ward, I spotted these bizarre, enormous art fishes suspended from the ceiling. I used to adore these as a kid! Their names were Daddy, Mummy, and Sophie. My mother used to drop me up at the radio station and return at a predetermined time to pick me up. As I recall, there were a few people in the room.

I noticed microphones, people wearing headphones, and a lot of equipment. Working in the radio department was a blast. It compelled me to break out in some way from my cocoon. I was able to forget about my problems thanks to the music, and I was able to enjoy every moment. The music that was always playing in my thoughts and the room was 'Agadoo.' I used to get caught up in the scene and sing along. It made them happy, laugh, and smile.

I feel that no matter how terrible your circumstances are and how helpless and frustrated you feel, you must always look on the bright side, find the silver lining to the cloud in order to survive, and hang on and never ever give up.

Eventually, I was discharged from the hospital when I no longer needed immediate medical attention or hospitalization. Although I went home with my bag, there was still a lot of back and forth to the hospital for things like bandage changes, blood tests, and even more surgeries. The distance between my home and the hospital was a lot, so my father drove me there because I had to keep coming back for surgeries and follow-up appointments. I was lucky to have brilliant plastic surgeons and orthopedics who looked after me throughout many years of my follow-up treatments.

When I was a kid, I dreamt of being a singer. I love singing, but the truth is that I am terrible at it. But I never let that get in the way of my dream. When my father took me to my countless hospital appointments, I would always sing in the car. In fact, my father used to call me "*Hannah Montana*" when I was well enough to prance around the house, my microphone in hand. What was amazing was that my father sang the Hannah Montana songs with me. He learnt the words because of my constant singing.

Hannah Montana was my ideal as a kid. I wanted to be like her. I could not wait to finish school, race home, run to the lounge and switch on the television to watch my favourite series. There were many things that I loved about her, but what I really adored was the father-daughter bond they highlighted. It is similar to what I have with my father, and I feel truly blessed by the strong bond that I share with him.

When my sister and I used to see our mother from time to time, we always did some impromptu karaoke. We acted and sang songs and had such a wonderful time together. Even today, while driving my own car, whenever I play music, I turn up the volume and sing at the top of my lungs.

I still hold a soft spot for Hannah Montanna, aka Miley Cyrus, but not the Miley you see today. If you listen to her earlier songs before her solo debut when she dropped the moniker of Hannah Montana, the lyrics are amazing; they made me feel alive.

I played her songs all the time, and they made me feel good. It's probably why, whenever I feel sad or upset, I naturally turn towards music. It helps me when I sing, and it makes me feel better. They say music is therapy for the soul, and I really believe that.

If you listen to Miley Cyrus now, you realise just how different she sounds from her former self and how her lyrics have completely changed. Now her songs have more worldly themes, apart from love, family, and happiness. She completely changed from what she used to be. I guess it is because she got older. In reality, people do change with time. No one stays the same.

When I had to endure the long commute to the hospital and the painful treatments awaiting me there, one thing that I really looked forward to was getting to meet my nan and grandad afterward. I had a broken family life, but my grandparents were always there for me, and over the years, I have stayed really close to them.

Once I was better, my father took me back to the same

school I had attended before falling ill. It felt so weird being the odd one out, left on the sidelines. I felt sad because I could see other kids running around, playing games, skipping rope, and using the swings. I could not run because I was the only one in a wheelchair. I did have a playtime carer who came around from time to time and would interact with me and give me company. But I still found it difficult to adjust to my old school.

After some time, my father realised that I was having a tough time. Although I tried not to complain, he pulled me out of my old school and put me in a different school.

I have been through so much, and when readers turn the pages of my book, I know people will be blown away. It is true that I have lived life at a fast pace, so sometimes I feel really old, but I am only 29. But that does not even begin to tell you what kind of a life I have lived at such a breakneck pace.

There is a struggle in everyone's life; no one's life is perfect. But everyone has a dream to follow, some people can get there, and some fall by the wayside. Since I was in my teens, I have always had a dream like other girls. But there were a lot of ups and downs in my family, which affected me badly. A lot of stuff got in the way, and I found myself lost in the struggle to achieve my dreams and aspirations. Sometimes I reached my goals, but then something would go wrong or stop me.

# Kaylie Louise

*"Resilience is accepting your new reality even if it's less good than the one you had before. You can fight it, you can do nothing but scream about what you've lost, or you can accept that and try to put together something that's good."*

-Elizabeth Edwards

Life has its ups and downs, but you need to keep going and never stop fighting; that is what I have been doing for so long. Do not think that you are the only one going through the struggle. I want to let you know that you are not alone. Just keep trying, and do not give up.

By sharing my personal journey, I hope you can see that one lesson stands out - always have the courage to keep moving ahead, no matter how scary and treacherous the path ahead may be. Living in this world is hard, and along the way, you will lose your dreams, hope, love, health, and success. But that does not mean you should give up. The moment you lose hope, your spirit will die, and then it will be downhill from there.

I like to think I am a fighter, believing in myself, holding on to hope, and moving forward. Look at me. I cannot even explain how I am standing here today after all that I have been through, but all I know is that you just have to keep going—one foot after another.

Do not look back because then you will become distracted

and lose your direction. It is easy to get enmeshed or trapped in the past. I still do. But I have to somehow find a way to deal with the circumstances that come my way in the present to build the future I want. My past will never go away; it will always be with me. All I can do is to accept it and move on to the present.

I would like to share my slogan and mantra for life with my readers.

*"Pain in life can feel devastating, and all that you want is for it to just fly away or for someone else to come and take it away. You should always remember your loved ones. Do not let them suffer along with you. Show yourself as strong and a winner.'*

-Kaylie Louise

# Chapter 4
# The Special School Experience

The first word in the phrase *"special children"* refers to a child's *"special needs,"* not to the child being gifted. Unfortunately, even though it is the second word in *"special needs"* that matters the most, these very same needs are often overlooked by the people around them.

However, my father figured out early that I needed to go to a different kind of school, considering my needs. Consequently, he had no qualms about admitting me to a new school that would accommodate me in this area. Despite this, I was saddened by this decision because I would have to leave behind my favourite classmates and teachers, but more than sadness, it was anxiety. I was anxious because I couldn't understand why he was putting me in a different kind of school.

Now I believe it was a rational decision and the best one for me at the time. Suppose a child has a learning impairment or a condition that makes it difficult to do what most children their age are able to accomplish. In that case, it is clear that they have special educational needs.

They may be experiencing difficulties with traditional

schooling, whether it relates to their communication, learning, or social skills. In such cases, the help of specialists, instructors, and non-profit organizations that focus on this area can be invaluable. They can also assist and advise the parents to make sound decisions for the future of their child. I got this notion later on in my life.

Special classes for specially-abled children are an absolute necessity. Individual learning allows students to enjoy their studies and acquire confidence at their own pace. It removes the pressure of having the child conform to the pace of the classroom and believe that something is wrong with them when they're unable to do so. All special children must receive appropriate education for their personal growth and development. They may have sensory or physical needs that impact their academic performance.

A student may be affected by various impairments, including *Autism Spectrum Disorder, Multiple Disabilities, Developmental Delay, Traumatic Brain Injury, Orthopedic Impairment, Speech and Language Impairment, Visual and Hearing Impairment* (including blindness), and others. Emotional, mental, physical, and developmental disabilities can all be overcome with the children being given alternate possibilities that allow them to thrive.

In most cases, a school can assist by ensuring that they have the right professionals in their team for children with special needs.

If a child has special educational needs, they may require additional assistance with their schoolwork and simple things like reading, writing, math, comprehension, expressing themselves positively, making friends, interacting with adults, behaving appropriately in school, and organising themselves.

My father was doing all this for me, but I was very nervous about the new class and teachers. Regardless, the first day of school arrived, and saying goodbye to my father after he dropped me off was the hardest thing for me at that moment. Upon reaching the room, the teacher bent down and said hello to me, to which I replied courteously.

Apparently, the new school was actually interesting. There were amazing paintings, stories, and pictures on the classroom walls, which attracted me as a child. Special children like me progress at different rates and have different ways in which they learn best. When planning lessons, my teacher used to consider this by looking carefully at how I responded in the classroom and took to my lessons books and other materials.

It is important to mention that in the initial days of my new school, I faced a social problem; bullying. I was bullied terribly by a pupil from another class. Yes, he wasn't even my classmate, but he used to bully me terribly every day. Every other day at school became a nightmare for me, and I always wanted to skip school so that I would not have to face him again. Even when my father dropped me at school forcefully, I would cry in the girl's bathroom for hours and wish to magically escape from the school.

While a certain person from another class was horrible to me, my teachers at school were very supportive. The teacher would choose suitable ways to help me learn. Even though I was making slow progress and having problems in many areas, they provided me with extra help or different lessons to help me succeed.

Nonetheless, my progress was slow because of the bullying I was receiving. It got to the point where the teachers informed my father that I was progressing slower than expected in my studies and activities, despite their help. It was all due to the bullying. As soon as I reached the school, my heart would start pounding, and I wanted to hide somewhere to avoid being ridiculed every day.

Bullying is a severe problem that many children have to face in their schools, regardless of whether they are special needs or not. Some may dismiss it as a normal part of school life, but for many children, it creates mental and physical suffering that leaves scars on their psyche; in extreme situations, it can even lead to suicidal behaviour.

Schools must accept responsibility and improve their response to the crisis. Bullying has significant educational consequences, and students who are bullied frequently experience higher levels of stress, which can lead to a reduced ability to learn. As a result, there is more absenteeism and poor performance, as seen by lower exam scores.

I was also extremely disheartened to the point where I was considering suicide as the way out. I didn't want to cry for long hours in the bathroom and didn't want to attend school at all. The bullying was making me hate that place. Sometimes I wished for the bully to disappear magically, and sometimes I considered taking my own life to end the everyday torture.

The new school and the gifts it came with meant nothing when my confidence was shattering in it. The bullying made me feel my illness and disability more. While I was struggling at my new school, I found out that two of my close friends had passed away. This event further added to the misery I was going through, and it was a very depressing experience altogether. One day, it felt like I was at a point in my life where I had to stand up for myself. I had suffered enough at the hands of this boy who was a bully. Throughout all the years, till I reached Year 11, the bully would still appear. I felt he was always getting away with situations.

I didn't understand why or how, given his record, he ended up staying in the school. When I was in Year 10, one day at school, I felt like I wanted to fight back. My father taught me to stand up for myself and not let anyone upset me. He also suggested that I should go to another school, but I did not want to do that. I wanted to be brave and not let this one person scare me away.

After that fateful confrontation when I put him in his place, I felt strong and proud of myself. I was not scared of the bully anymore. I started enjoying school, and I made him realise that his actions did not bother me anymore. I could see in his eyes that he didn't like it. He felt defeated. Eventually, he became more distant and finally left me alone. For me, it was not simple or short progress. It took a long time and was a constant struggle for me to get to this stage.

Now I want to bust this myth for you. Yes, children also experience depression. Childhood depression is distinct from the *"blues"* and other common emotions that adults experience or the teenage angst one goes through as one grows up. Furthermore, just because a child appears unhappy doesn't indicate that they're suffering from depression.

However, my anxiety and sorrow persisted and adversely affected my social activities, interests, academics, and family life. It was just an indication that I was suffering from a depressive disorder. Remember that while depression is a serious condition, it is also one that can be treated.

I had my own fears and worries and felt sad and hopeless from time to time. These started appearing at different times during school. Furthermore, I was taken to the orthopedics again because my bones were not growing properly, and the doctor advised multiple surgeries for treatment.

My little self was dealing with many burdens at such a

young age - bullying, loss of close friends, illness, and now another thing was added to the bucket of problems. I was still trying to get better and to get out of the depression only for my father, as he was trying everything that was in his capacity to make me feel better.

Months passed by, and finally, the day of my surgery arrived. As I hit my teens, I was a girl drowned in depression and surrounded by miseries. I was ready to undergo surgery despite being scared. I was terrified by the idea of getting metal plates in my leg. The doctor told my father that I wouldn't be able to walk for at least a few months as it was a slow process. The body takes a lot from the rest of skeleton and muscles to repair the injury in such a situation.

The next day after the surgery, I opened my eyes but was not able to look around. I felt weak; I couldn't move my hands or feel my left leg even after trying two to three times. The metal implant surgery was done, and I was lying on the hospital bed helplessly waiting for my father to show up. A few minutes later, my father came into the room; glancing at him made me feel better. That day I knew that my actual test in patience had just started. I had to wait for months to walk on my legs without help.

When dealing with a crisis, it's tough to believe that the situation will eventually lead to some kind of progress; that's how I felt after the surgery. The ability to bounce back from hardship and grow from the experience is referred to as resilience.

In fact, experts discovered in a study that people who experienced a moderate level of adversity had improved mental health and well-being and higher life satisfaction over time than those who had no history of adversity. I had no idea in which category of experiencing hardships I fell into at the time of my surgery.

# Chapter 5
# The Childhood Dream

*"Without leaps of imagination or dreaming, we lose the excitement of possibilities. Dreaming, after all, is a form of planning. "*

-Gloria Steinem

Dreams, plans, and ambitions, we all have them. From a very young age, I used to dream about many things that I could be. But, like many other kids, my dreams and goals changed every other day. One day I would want to be a model, and the next day I would wish to become a designer. I can't even remember all the goals I had imagined for myself.

But, there is this one childhood dream of mine that I distinctly remember to this day. Even though I never achieved or pursued it, I still consider it a part of my safe space. From a young age, I wanted to become a singer. I found songs and music as an escape from my worries and my troubles, even if it was for a little while, and that was enough to give me mental peace.

As a child, my musical dream was all I could think about. Apart from all the problems and burdens I was facing, I found my dreams and my goals as my haven. I always listened carefully to all the lyrics of the songs. Some songs depicted perfectly what I was going through or how I was feeling; some days, I listened to those on repeat. I always felt a connection to music and songs. Even now and then, whenever I am feeling low, I always find music as my escape.

Even though I loved listening to songs and I loved singing, I was, and I still am, a terrible singer.

As a kid, I always looked up to people, people who had amazing voices and who could sing really well, people who were attending musical schools, and celebrities who were famous for their hit songs. So in my free time, I would open my computer, and I loved to do my research on them and used to get excited by reading the journeys and success stories of famous singers. I always thought and dreamt that I, too, would be a great singer one day, and my profile would also be displayed on the internet, just like the rest of them.

Becoming a singer was a childhood dream that I got so involved in. I believed in myself to sing at the top of my lungs and could think of nothing else as my profession. Until I realised something - I am so bad at singing.

If you think I have a beautiful voice and I could write some amazing heartfelt song, no, I don't. In fact, I believe that I have a terrible voice and I don't sing well at all. I like the fact that I believed in my spirit of happiness when I sang. Whenever I sang, my partner would look at me from time to time, and I always wondered why he was laughing. One day, when I was doing the dishes and singing one of my favourite songs, I asked him why he would always smile looking at me. He told me that he couldn't believe how I get my emotions into the songs as I sing.

Here is how the thought of becoming a singer came to my mind as a child. As my father and we were almost always on the road, traveling here and there for hospital visits, surgeries, checkups, and whatnot, we used to listen to a lot of songs. All of the popular songs by *Hannah Montana* would be on our car radio every single day. We listened to her so much that we learnt all the lyrics of all of her songs. I loved her.

The older I got, the closer I grew closer to my father. I would surely give some of the credit to all those car rides that we would take to the hospital visits and all those songs we sang together. As a kid, I shared everything with my father. I would love to share what happened all day at school and everything else I did. Many kids hesitate to share their thoughts, dreams, and ambitions with their parents. But I loved to share all these with my father, particularly because he was an excellent listener and always believed in me. My father always supported me in all my decisions; he stood there like a rock when things went down for me.

My father's support in all those difficult stages of my life has resulted in me being very confident in myself and in everything that I do in life. I know he would be there, standing, cheering me up in whatever I try to accomplish in my life. It is only because of my father's encouragement that today I can stand up for myself.

As I have mentioned earlier that I admired and loved Hannah Montana so much when I was young; I wanted to be just like her. I loved how she dressed as Hannah Montana, that straight blonde wig she wore with bangs covering her forehead, all those colourful dresses and jackets, and the funky jewelry pieces that she wore. I used to adore all of that, and I wanted to be as same as her.

I would sing Hannah Montana songs all day long. Even when I was doing house chores like doing the dishes, folding my laundry, or cleaning my bedroom, you would always find me humming Hannah Montana songs. Even though I loved all of her songs, my favourite ones were *"Nobody's Perfect," "Best of Both Worlds," "The Climb,"* and *"True Friend."* I still remember these songs and their lyrics perfectly.

Every day, the moment after my father had dropped me off at school, I would count down the hours so that I could get back home and watch TV. The moment I would get back home from school, I used to turn the TV on and watch *The Hannah Montana TV series.* For me, it was the best time of the day. I would forget all my worries and pains and laugh along with all the jokes of the series that Hannah and her best friend, Lilly Truscott made. And I would sing along to all of the songs, which were already stuck in my mind and which I used to hum all day long.

Apart from the love I had for Hannah Montana and her songs, I liked watching the series because of the father-daughter bond that she had in the series. That bond reminded me of the bond that my father and I shared. A perfect father-daughter duo - which is what I have with my father. I loved the fact that I could share anything and everything with my father. Not many kids have that relationship with their fathers, but I did, and I am so happy about that.

With all those hospital visits and surgeries, and checkups, I had my father by my side. No matter what I wanted to do, even if it was something foolish or crazy, he would always be the first one to say yes. My father supported me through the worst times of my life, and I am so grateful for that.

On the car rides, we would sing along to Hannah Montana every single day. We had all of her songs remembered by heart. The car rides that I and my father shared were the best.

Even though my dream never became a reality, being a singer and enjoying singing was still the best dream that I had as a child. I never actually thought of becoming a singer when I grew up because I know I am a terrible, terrible singer. So I would record myself singing and would cringe after listening to the tapes. I don't know how my father and my sister tolerated me all those years when I used to sing a song on repeat the whole day.

My sister and I live with our father because he won custody of us over our mother. So it was agreed upon that we would live with our father on the weekdays and go and live with our mother on the weekends.

So, on the weekends, my father would drive us to our mother's flat. She lived a little far from our father's house, so it took a while for us to get there. When my sister and I got older, we started driving. We would usually take turns driving to our mother's. On the way, me and my sister enjoyed singing together. We had so much fun; people on the road would smile and wave when they would look at us singing.

My sister is also fond of music. No, she never wanted to be a singer, not that I know of. She did play guitar from time to time, though, and she was pretty good at it. So we would turn the music on in full volume, and we would sing our lungs out along with the songs. We also did little karaoke sessions. Singing all of our favourite songs one by one, we had the best time. We also acted to the songs, and we would have fits of laughter looking at each other.

There were times we did karaoke at our mother's flat on weekends. Our mother also got us the karaoke speakers, along with two microphones, and she would record us singing and dancing. She also got the disco ball out, so it felt like being on stage! She used to dress us up and do our make-up, and I remember I loved having sparkly eyes. We played our songs, and my sister and I would sing our hearts out. I remember when I reached my teens, one day, she found a tape recording of us. We asked her to play it, and so she did. When she played it, you could hear my sister and I singing the Titanic song, '*My Heart Will Go On*.' It made us cringe as we couldn't believe how we sounded at that time. But it was cute to hear and look at our moments together at the same time. Those were the best times to call mother and sister bond.

My sister and I had been through so much just when we were little kids. We saw our family falling apart, and all those traumas that we saw of our mother's boyfriends made us scared of everything.

The entire trauma, the bad memories, the pain and sufferings that I went through, we forgot it all in those car rides. It was just me, my sister and some good songs. That is what music is to me, my sweet escape. From that moment on, and 29 years later, I still remember all those lyrics and the feelings that music gave me.

I know I am an awful singer, but still, to this day, whenever I am driving my car, I would turn on the music to a loud volume and sing along the songs, and to this day, this childhood dream of mine makes me happy.

# Chapter 6
# It Gets Harder

Being sick was all I remember since I was a child. I felt weak all the time, I would throw up every day, and I was in the hospital more than I was in my own home. I remember crying with every pain that I was feeling. I have been going in and out of the operation theatre since I was seven years old.

When I was little, I didn't know much about what was happening to me and why I was getting all those needles and tubes inside me. I just remember being very sick from the start. I just remember all the post-operation pain from the surgeries that was so much for me as a child; I was unable to bear it sometimes.

My father and mother were always there to comfort me after every surgery. They would play with me, talk to me and try to do anything to divert my mind off the pain and discomfort I felt after each surgery. Especially when I was a child, both my parents would be there. It was only when I began to live with my father, who had the responsibility to take me to all my appointments and surgeries. My father was there the most. There were times when my mother and father would be together with me at the hospital to give me support. Once I reached my teens, it would only be my father and I. My father came across as the tough one. I know deep down how devasted he felt watching me like that, but he's my rock. He taught me to be tough, as that's in his nature. My nan and grandad were also always there for me. I remember asking my father to take me to see my grandparents before taking me to my hospital appointments. I was really close with my nan and grandad.

The number of surgeries increased as I grew older. I was now experiencing things that I never understood as a child. Whenever I had surgery, my father would bribe me, and he made it all seem so easy. I went with the flow with every surgery and every appointment that I had. As I grew older, it all started making sense to me. I knew exactly what was wrong with me, which I never really got when I was seven years old.

I knew what the doctors talked about, the risk factors and how they will proceed with the operation; it would send chills down my spine. I was not able to sleep, and I experienced insomnia weeks before my scheduled surgery. I also developed anxiety due to my illness and all those constant surgeries. I was not able to eat anything, and I remember feeling scared all the time. Whenever I got back home after my doctor's appointment, I would feel very anxious. I would always be upset and in a bad mood.

Each surgery would leave me more and more emotional. I was in a constant battle with my own emotions. Sometimes I felt calm, and the very next moment, I would be on the verge of crying.

I was so scared all the time. I was always anxious at every doctor visit, scared that they would schedule me for another surgery. Even I couldn't understand why I would cry in the middle of the night. Or when someone tried to comfort me after or before my surgery, I would start crying hysterically.

Other days, I would get upset for no reason at all, even when I was feeling just fine. I guess that was post-surgery depression, which is very common in most people. I also lost interest in almost all activities that I liked. I remember days when I didn't even feel like listening to music, which was my favourite escape. Surgeries had taken a severe toll on my mental health. I started developing anxiety and depression from a very young age because of that.

From the start, everything has always been hard for me. One day, after a regular appointment with my doctor, I was advised to turn to Orthopedics, as the doctors were concerned about my bones. As a child, I was diagnosed with Meningitis Septicemia. Because of this illness, I went through a lot of surgeries. All those surgeries affected my bones. The reports showed that my bones were not growing properly or as they should. Over time, I had gone through many surgeries on my legs, leaving them scarred from all places. I had so much metal inside of me; that I started to feel like a Bionic Woman.

In one of my surgeries, the doctors inserted a metal plate in my lower left leg. After a while, the metal started sticking out, and my father would help me turn the nozzle every time. I was not quite healed from this surgery, and the doctors scheduled another bone surgery for me. In the next one, they had to insert a metal plate again on the side of my left leg.

The doctors explained the whole procedure to my father and me. I remember being so scared that time. I was tear-eyed the entire time. My orthopedic doctor also informed me that they would have to do another surgery to take the metal plate out later. Hearing this made me more frightened than I already was.

I was done being ill. I kept praying and thinking on each doctor visit that this would be my last surgery. But unfortunately, that didn't happen for me.

A few years later, the metal plate which the doctors inserted in my left leg started getting uncomfortable for me. In the start, my leg felt heavy sometimes, and it would itch and hurt a little. The pain was still bearable for me.

A few weeks later, the metal plate in my leg was giving me sharp shooting pains. It would hurt a lot; I remember I could not sleep because of the pain in my left leg. My father and I went to see my doctor, and she suggested that it was time that the metal plate should come out. So, as scared as I was of any more surgeries, I had another surgery to remove the metal plate from my leg.

I had surgery about five years back, where the doctors had to insert another metal plate in my right leg. I have to admit that these surgeries were getting harder and harder as I grew older. At the age when girls play with their toys and go to parks, I constantly visited hospitals. All this trauma and stress affected my mental health a lot.

Even to this day, I remember every single surgery and every pain that I experienced. I still have several problems with my legs. Some days they would feel fine, and the next day, I would feel like I couldn't even stand up on my own.

My sister and I were very young when our father won custody of us. We moved in with him at that time. At that age, we never really understood why we started living with our father instead of our mother. Even though I hated my mother's boyfriend, I still sometimes wondered why we moved in here with our father. I was too little to understand the law and court terms and agreements, so I went with the flow.

My father and I developed a very good bond over time. He was there for me when I was sick. I remember him being around in every surgery and my doctor's appointment. He would make us laugh, cook for us, and would spend all of his free time with us. The fact that our father would do anything for us made me more comfortable living in his place. I started liking living with my father, and I enjoyed being there.

But there were days when I still wondered why we ended up living with him and not my mother after they separated. I still hated my mother's boyfriend, but I missed her. As I grew up, I started understanding a lot of things that I didn't as a child. I was an inquisitive child from the start. I remember bombarding my father with questions. I would ask him why we lived with him and not our mother and all the different questions I had in my little mind. I was happy living with him, but the fact that I was not with my mother was still hurting me. I remember I felt the same way when I was living with my mother; I would miss my father a lot. But in my head, I knew I was in a better place. There was no other way. Both my parents had separated, and I had to live with one of my parents. Due to all the circumstances, I knew my father was the better option for us to live with.

When my mother and father separated, we had initially lived with our mother. I remember both of them fighting and yelling at each other over us. When my sister and I started living at his place, my father filed for our custody in court.

Our father won the case, and the court decided that my sister and I would live with him. The judge also decided that we would visit our mother on the weekends. So my sister and I would live at my father's house on the weekdays. On the weekends, my father would drive us to our mother's flat. When my sister learnt how to drive a car and had her license, we would go together there.

Our mother lived at a distance from our house. My sister would drive us there every weekend. After a while, I learnt to drive with a specialist instructor and was driving on the road too!

My sister and I always had fun on the car rides. Even when my father used to drop us off, we would really enjoy going there. Weekends at my mother's flat were always a fun time for us. It would be the three of us hanging out in her place.

We would discuss everything and tell each other what was going on in our lives. Like me, my mother also loved music. So we would dance and sing songs; she even got us a karaoke speaker. My sister and I loved playing dress-up as a game. It would always take my mind off my anxiety and health issues.

My mother loved dressing us up. She would put make-up on us. She even had all of our old childhood photographs and videos. She always kept it in a safe place. We looked at ourselves and our precious memories even though some of the photos made us cringe. So every weekend, we would take out some of the old videos and photos, and we had the best time at our mother's place. This does not mean I had no fun at my father's. I loved it there too. We spent so much time together, playing games and listening to music. I had so much fun with both parents. I'm glad to be living with my father, and I was happy to still see my mother from time to time.

I still do have leg problems. Sometimes they would hurt so

bad, and other days, I feel fine. I had my last surgery about five years back, and I still go through the same anxiety that I experienced as a child. My illness made me weak, and I was not always active, but I am glad that I had my parent's support with me. They helped me get through that rough phase of my life.

# Chapter 7
# College and Relationships

Going into college can be very challenging and uncertain for a person. Sometimes, people haven't decided on their careers when they start college. Or sometimes, they don't even have an idea what they are doing. Relationships can also sometimes give a hard time. As you grow up, there are many things that you need to figure out, and that feeling can turn out very overwhelming at times.

When I was about to go to college, I was very nervous. I felt anxious because it was my first time deciding where I wanted to study further. I did all my research before applying; I wanted my college process to be very smooth. I didn't really look at a lot of colleges. I chose one that was close to home, so I didn't have to travel far. Also, I liked the look of the building. It was modernistic and suited my type.

I was very hesitant before my semester started. I had always been to special schools due to my health issues and constant surgeries, so going to a regular college was a little different for me. But, as much as I was nervous, I was also excited at the same time. I was looking forward to starting the next phase of my life. I was excited to explore my options and choose what I wanted to study further. For the first time in my entire life, I felt like I was in control of what I was doing. It was all still new to me, but I was ecstatic.

I still remember my first day of college. I was too anxious that I couldn't sleep properly that night. I also woke up early in the morning. I also couldn't eat my breakfast properly; I was so nervous that it made me nauseous. I was thinking about my first day in college all the time. I had so many questions in my mind. My father sensed that I was nervous, and he tried to calm me down, and it always worked. I felt a little calm after talking to him.

Have you ever had first-day anxiety?

As I reached the college building, my anxiety and nervousness crept up again. There were new people and new faces; everything was unknown at that point. I was always a bright student from the start. I liked to study to learn about new things. But when it was time to choose a subject in my college, I had no idea what I should do next.

After much research and giving it a lot of thought, I decided to take up ICT as my subject. I was always interested in technology, and I felt like I was good at ICT. However, even after taking ICT, I was not entirely sure what I wanted to do in the future. But at that time, ICT felt like a sane option for me, so I enrolled in it.

For me, college ended up being nice. At the start, I felt very nervous and anxious going there, but as soon as I started talking to my classmates, I started enjoying college. I made a lot of friends in college. I became friends with everyone in the class. I had a group, and in it, I was the only girl! I loved it. I was very passionate about studying hard and getting good grades. College was the time for me to take control of my life better and start to feel stronger.

I did not have much confidence being at school. I did not know how to feel. I was still trying to accept myself for who I was. I had friends at school, but college turned out better for me. I felt stronger being there. I felt happier to finish school and start a fresh beginning. After going through the exhaustion of all those surgeries, this change felt nice to me. I started to gain my confidence back. I was happy again.

Throughout college, I had more guy friends than girlfriends. I realised that I got along with guys more than I did with girls. I had many girlfriends, but I felt more comfortable with guys. I think it was because my father brought me up.

In college, I would hang out with all of my guy friends more in our free time. We would sit around the college campus all the time. We also did many group studies together, and it would always end up being a gaming party instead of a group study.

I made a lot of good memories in college. Those were indeed the best years of my life. But the best part of college was my best friend. We didn't talk for a few classes when I joined. He was quiet and kept himself to himself. One day, I turned up slightly late for class, and I had to find a seat to sit down. I sat next to him because I thought it would be nice to get to know him. Once we started talking, we got on really well. We shared everything. I felt so comfortable talking to him about my health, studies, family, and everything.

Even to this day, I am still in touch with him. He is my best friend, and I am just as close to him now as I was before.

It was hard to live with just one parent. We would miss our mother when we were at our father's house on the weekdays. And we missed our father when we would be with our mother. From the start, I wanted a serious relationship.

I wanted someone who I could share all my feelings with, my happiness and sadness. I wanted someone who would support me and comfort me through my medical checkups and surgeries. I wished to have someone I would love and spend the rest of my life with. I wanted to be loved, and I wanted to be able to follow my dreams.

I saw many couples totally in love in college, and I felt so happy watching them together. My future plans were straight and clear for me from the start. I knew I wanted a healthy relationship with the person I love. I wanted to have a big family, so we all could be there with each other through thick and thin. I wanted a big house, a happy marriage, and a successful career. I knew what I wanted, and I had my heart set on my dreams. But I couldn't be grateful for how my life turned out.

I was a serious student throughout my college. My studies and my grades were my top priority. I used to study day and night, and I scored well in almost all of my subjects. I wanted a successful career, and I was content that I was working towards it. Between all of this, I would also go for my medical checkups with my father every now and then. When I was in school, I let my surgeries and my illness take the best of me. But this time, I made sure to concentrate solely on my studies. I didn't let my health issues get in between my career goals. I wanted to be successful in the future, and I was certain of it.

Throughout college, I had some short-lived, non-serious relationships. It was clear that I wanted to be with someone I really loved, but I hadn't found anyone in college just yet. Mostly in those relationships, both of us were not serious with each other, and our relationship would end over the pettiest thing.

I remember; there was this guy in college. He was one of my classmates. We became friends first, and I liked him at first. He was funny. He made me laugh with his jokes and silly pranks. He had amazing eyes, ones that you could easily fall for. So, we started talking. After some time, he confessed that he liked me. I always liked him, so I agreed, and we started dating. The first couple of months were amazing. He made me laugh a lot. I remember he would say the silliest things, and I would break into fits of laughter. He would listen to my endless stories, and he also gave the best advice. Things were going really well between us.

After some good months of us being together, he suddenly started acting strange. He would not sit with me, even when I asked. He also stopped joking around with me, which once made me laugh. I asked what was wrong with him several times, but we would always end up in a huge argument. This went on for some weeks, but I couldn't figure out what was wrong with him.

One day, one of my other guy friends came over to me. He told me that my boyfriend was having an affair with someone else. It came to me as a shock at first. Just when I started liking him, he ended up having another affair. My friend also told me a few home truths, which made me believe it. My friend was nothing like my boyfriend. He wasn't ridiculously funny, silly, and well-spoken. I confronted my boyfriend about this, but he denied all of this in an instant. Eventually, the relationship just ended. During the arguments, I started hanging out with one of my group members from class again. He didn't like it. But I knew I deserved to be with someone better who would treat me with respect.

A few days later, the same friend who told me about my ex-boyfriend's affair asked me out. I was not sure at first because we were excellent friends, but he convinced me somehow, and we started going out. It was a casual relationship, and things were going just fine, but we both realised that we were better off as friends.

There was another guy that I was in a relationship with. He was also from my college. He was a nice guy, so when he asked me out, I said yes. We started dating, but it seemed like I was always the one waiting for him. He was also doing a job with his studies, so he was busy there almost all the time, and the rest of the time, he would study. We both barely talked because of his busy schedule. I wanted someone who could make time for me, at least. I ignored it all at first, but I couldn't take it anymore after a few weeks. I was tired of waiting around for him all the time. He would arrive late or just cancel out at the last minute if we had some plans together. So, I ended that relationship also.

I was in and out of several relationships in college, but none of them were serious ones. I was clear about what I wanted in a relationship. I never let those short-lived relationships get in between my studies or my peace of mind. I wanted a successful career, and I was working hard to achieve it. It was enough for me at that time.

# Chapter 8
# The College Dream

*"You are never given a dream without also being given the power to make it come true. You will have to work for it, however."*

-Richard Bach

Every person in this world has their dreams, their own goals, and missions. From an early age, people make up their minds on what they want to be when they grow up. Even though sometimes those dreams might sound silly, a person needs to have their own dreams and goals for their future. Dreams inspire us to be better people and work hard for what we have thought for ourselves. They give you a direction, and they give your life a purpose.

Working towards something you always thought for yourself surely is hard. You will have many difficulties along the way, but once you accomplish your dream and your goals, you will have immense satisfaction and pride in yourself.

Unfortunately, not all dreams come true. People often feel sad and depressed after they couldn't achieve what they were working so hard for. I am no stranger to failure. I know how it feels. But the truth is, it is not the end. There are endless opportunities out there. You just have to motivate yourself to move ahead.

I believe that there is no right time or limit to set a new goal for yourself. You just have to believe in yourself no matter what. And you will be surprised at the things you could accomplish.

Since I was a little girl, I have had so many dreams for myself. The very first one I had was that I wanted to become a singer. I enjoyed listening to music, and I loved singing along with it. Even though I knew I sounded very bad, I still wanted to sing. I always felt like I could relate to the lyrics of certain songs, and it made me feel passionate about my feelings and experiences.

When I went to college, my singing dream was long gone. At that point, I was grown enough to understand that I could never be a singer. Yes, I still sing all of my favourite songs in the shower or when I am driving and doing the dishes, almost all the time to be honest, but I have no dream now of becoming a singer. When I think about it, I laugh at myself for my silly singing dream.

As I grew up, deciding what I would do in the future or what to take as a profession was hard for me. I didn't know what I should take as my subject. I looked into my options, and after a lot of thought, I chose ICT; it was a hard decision because my entire career was dependent on what I would take.

But still, I was always good at my studies, and I was confident in my decision; I knew I could do it. I enjoyed studying ICT. Mostly because I made so many friends there, and I had an amazing group of friends; we all had so much fun every single day. I enjoyed ICT, I was good at the subject, and I got good grades on all of my projects. So I was satisfied with my decision to choose ICT as my major.

I always loved reading magazines. Whenever I went out, I would grab a magazine for myself to read at home. I was more interested in stacking them up on my bookshelf rather than reading them all. I was always fascinated by the magazine covers and the attractive images and content. They always grabbed my attention, and I would be compelled to buy them.

All those bold colours, attractive images, and different patterns enchanted me the most. I would always think about the person who would do all this creative and innovative work on every magazine so that every person was bound to pick one out of pure attraction. So I would buy one or two magazines every time I went out.

Slowly, I started to become more and more interested in magazine designing. I wanted to be a Magazine Designer. However, my new interest was making me confused and left me doubting my decision to take ICT in the first place. By that time, I was two years in ICT, but my interest was now elsewhere to my surprise. At first, I brushed my thoughts off. I thought doing ICT would be better for me and my career. And so I continued my classes as usual. But as my interest grew in becoming a Magazine Designer, I was not able to ignore it anymore. And so, I decided to do something about it.

I knew many of my friends who were confused about their majors; they went to see a Career Advisor so they could make the right decision. So, I decided to see a Career Advisor too.

After a while, I found myself sitting with the Career Advisor. I was really hoping that it would help me choose between ICT and a Magazine Designer. I had a lengthy discussion with my Career Advisor. We discussed the different subjects that I would have to take and how different Magazine Designing is from ICT. We also discussed the scope that Magazine Designers have in these times. She asked me what I wanted to do and where my interest was the most. After discussing all the possible factors for a while, she advised me to go into Art and Design to get my qualifications in that area.

I let out a sigh of relief when she told me that I should be a Magazine Designer. Of course, I was hoping for the same result, and that was it. But in the end, she told me that it was entirely up to me what I wanted to do and what I wanted to be. So, I was satisfied with my Career Advisor's suggestion, but I still had a lot of thinking to do.

I was two years into ICT, and I liked it there too. However, leaving ICT was one of the hardest decisions that I ever made. I had an amazing group of friends in ICT. Good friends are very hard to find, and I was lucky to have a group of the most amazing friends there. We all were very close to each other, we laughed at the stupidest things, and we all got along easily. My amazing friends were another reason why it was hard for me to leave ICT and choose another major.

But despite everything, I had to put my priorities straight and keep the future in my mind. I have always dreamt of having a successful career. I always wanted to do something that I loved doing, and at that time, going into Art and Design seemed like a sensible choice to me.

So, I made a decision and left ICT after two good years. And then, I started my course in Art and Design. I liked studying there. I always had an interest in creativity, arts, and designs, so I enjoyed it there. My grades were coming out well, and my interest in Magazine Designing grew day by day. I was excited to finish college and to start designing some cool and creative magazines. I dreamt of my designed magazines on the book store's shelves, and I felt like I was close to accomplishing it.

After a year of studying Art and Design, I started sending letters to Magazine Companies. I would send my application, requesting an Apprenticeship in every Magazine Company that I could find. I waited eagerly for their response. Every morning when I woke up, I would check my emails, hoping for a reply. Unfortunately, all the confidence that I had at the start of my designing journey started coming down slowly.

I was so excited when I finished college. I had dreams that I would design covers and magazines and show my creative side to the world. But as days passed, I could feel my dreams crumble up. I never heard anything back from any of those Magazine companies. I was shattered. All of the hard work that I did in college was looking like a waste of effort for me. I regretted leaving ICT; I regretted all of the decisions that I made regarding my future. I didn't know what to do next. I had no other focus on what I wanted to do.

When I was a teenager, I started writing a story. I remember how good it was, and everyone who read it loved it. It took me a little while to finish that story, but I felt so good when I was finished with it. I loved it when my family and my friends praised me for my writing skills. I have always loved reading and writing. I remember buying all different notebooks whenever I went out.

I would write everything and anything. I collected certain books that fit my interests. Colourful notebooks were always piled up on my bookshelf, and I would write down a new story as soon as I was finished with the old one.

I knew that my dream of becoming a Magazine Designer would never come true, and I could feel it. I was devastated. Until one day, I had a new dream. I dreamt of writing a book. I always loved to write, and I loved to express myself in my words. I wanted people to read my stories and to know me as a successful writer. I wanted to get a book out to the world. My hopes went up again, and this time, I was sure I would succeed.

One day, I met up with a friend, and we planned to go out to grab a bite and do some shopping. After we were done with our lunch and shopping, we started rambling around. We walked past Waterstones, which is in Enfield. I couldn't help but notice so many books displayed through the glass window at a bookstore. I stopped there for a minute and looked at all those books beautifully sitting on the shelves.

"I want my book to be displayed like this," I said to my friend.

While I was standing in front of that bookstore, I dreamt of having my own book, my story to be displayed at all the bookstores. I knew there was no career for me in Magazines, and writing seemed like a great opportunity. I knew how to write wonderfully, and I knew how to convey my messages and thoughts through my words to the world. I had a gut feeling that I would be an amazing writer. So I decided to give writing a try that day. I decided to become a writer.

My friend pushed me and encouraged me so much to do it. She motivated me every step of the way. From that day on, I am still writing, and I love it. I love to write more than I loved being a Magazine Designer and more than the dream of becoming a singer.

I managed to get more involved in writing as time passed. I would spend hours thinking of new things and new stories that I could write. I have so much to tell the world, and I am happy that I chose to become a writer.

I never stopped when I was a child and always had a dream in my mind to follow. First, it was of becoming a singer, then a model. Then, there was a time when I wanted to become a designer too. After I failed to become a Magazine Designer, I followed another dream of mine. I became a writer, a pretty good one.

But, I didn't stop there; I still have many dreams and goals of mine. I have a dream of having a big beautiful house, a family, and a loving husband. But most of all, my dream is to be happy.

# Chapter 9
# Getting Serious

One of my dreams was to have a serious relationship where I could just be myself. I always wanted a big family of my own, with someone whom I love. For me, a serious relationship is something when being together with someone makes you feel at home. I never got this feeling with my boyfriends in college. Those relationships were hardly a month long. But I wanted something more. I wanted to be in a relationship with someone who would make time for me, love and respect me in every way possible.

I didn't like being in a short-lived relationship. I wouldn't say I liked how those ended for me. I was looking for someone whom I really liked. I wanted someone I could share everything with. Someone who would get me; and know what I want.

Luckily, I got one of my dreams to come true shortly after. In my life, I had three serious relationships. My first serious relationship started with a guy I met online. Meeting someone online was not very common at that time like it is nowadays. Whenever I told someone that I had met someone through the internet, they would look at me all startled like I had made a joke. So, he lived in Colchester.

That was a time when everyone used MSN Messenger. MSN became one of the most popular platforms for communication. We would talk on MSN, phone calls, and messages. Even though we met online, we had seen each other as we also talked through video calls all the time. No one really knew that I met him through the internet. I would lie and say that he came over once or met through mutual friends when someone asked.

Finally, I just told my mother the truth about him and that I met him online and we were dating. During the time that we were dating, both of us didn't know how to drive. So, we used to plan our meet-ups and travel by train. I met my boyfriend a couple of times in person too. He was a nice guy.

There was this one time that I went over to Colchester to meet his parents. He also introduced me to his friends. We were getting so involved with each other; that I believed that our relationship would last forever. I liked him a lot. I also invited him over to my place so he could meet my father. He met my mother when I first met him at the train station.

My father liked him too. That was the thing about him; he greeted everyone with so much respect that they started to like him in an instant. I was happy. My father didn't know how we met at that time. But once my father met him, I told him everything about our relationship and how we met.

We were together for a couple of months at this point. One day, when we were talking over the phone, we planned that he would stay a night with me. I thought I was ready. So, the next he came over, I was at my mother's flat. He stayed with me there. We talked and then started getting intimate with each other; that was my first sexual intercourse. I thought I was ready, but the truth was, I wasn't. When it all started happening, I felt like I was not ready, and I was being pushed into doing it. I still don't know why, but I felt like it was not right to do it with him.

Things were not the same for me after that night. I felt distant towards him. I thought it was just a phase and it will pass by. But as days passed, I realised that I didn't feel the same way towards him. It was like all my love and affection had been lost somewhere for him. I decided to talk to him about it. I can't live in a relationship where I felt like I was being pushed into, where I was not happy. I was supposed to go to Colchester a few weeks after and meet him. My suitcase was all packed, and everything was ready, but things changed. I called him when I was at my mother's and ended my relationship with him.

After a week or so, I felt unusual and not myself. I didn't feel good, so I decided to visit my doctor. The doctor did a smear test. I found out that I had caught an STI (Chlamydia).

I haven't been with anyone else except for him. I got scared as I knew nothing of what an STI was. So, I went home and researched all about it, its symptoms, and its risk factors. I read that if you don't treat an STI on time, you could develop fertility problems. So, I got treated for my STI right away. It went away after a few weeks, and I started feeling good again.

My second relationship was in 2009. We met through a mutual friend who also set us up on a date. We decided to meet after talking on the phone and messaging through MSN. For our first date, we went to the cinema to watch a movie. I fell in love with him straight away, even though it was just a first date. He was the perfect guy in every way.

After our first date, we planned to meet again. Every date got better and better than the last one. We realised that we were getting very serious with each other. We would talk for hours on the phone; there were nights when we would talk all night with each other. We shared everything. I told him everything about my previous relationships and how I got an STI.

One day, when we were talking on the phone, I asked him what he would do if I got pregnant. He was very straightforward about this topic. He said that if I got pregnant, I would have to get an abortion straight away. I was not expecting such an answer from him, but I ignored it anyway. Little did I know, my life was about to take a turn.

I was a little late, so I decided to take a pregnancy test, just in case. To my surprise, it came out positive. I didn't expect it to be positive, but it was. I stood there with the test in my hand; my mind was still processing it. I didn't tell anybody as I was too scared. I picked up my phone and called my boyfriend, and I told him the news with my hands still shaking.

I was just 17 years old at that time and was now pregnant. From our earlier conversation, he made it clear to me that if I got pregnant, I would have to abort it. That is what he said this time too. He asked me to get an abortion first thing in the morning. I didn't say anything because I had no other option. He said that he would leave me if I didn't go with the abortion. Again, I had no other option than to agree.

I went to the doctor to terminate my pregnancy. It was December of 2009. I expected that he would come with me. I expected him to support me in this difficult time, but he didn't come to the clinic. I needed him there. But, he was too concerned about the apprentice job that he chose to go to work that day rather than be with me.

I knew that he had told his sister about the pregnancy and the abortion. She came there with me to the clinic. She waited for me in the waiting area while I was called inside for the usual tests before the procedure. They took out my blood to check if I was actually pregnant. The results came out positive this time too. Later, they called me in for an ultrasound to check if everything was okay.

I remember lying there on the bed with so many doubts in my mind while the nurse did my ultrasound. Suddenly, I heard a heartbeat. It was my baby's heartbeat. I felt so emotional listening to it. It was the most soothing sound that I had heard. Tears welled up in my eyes as I looked at the screen.

I really wanted my boyfriend to be there for me and support me, but he wasn't. So I was all alone and scared. Only if it were up to me, I would have never gone with the abortion. But at that time, I felt like I had no choice. So, I had to terminate my pregnancy.

After the ultrasound, the nurse asked me to go upstairs and wait for a little while to prep everything for the procedure. I went upstairs to wait. In that waiting room, there were all pregnant ladies. My heart was crushed into a million pieces when I looked at them. I felt guilty about what I was going to do. I sat there, completely numb. After a while, they called out my name. I stood up and went to a room to change into a gown.

Once I changed into a gown, they asked me to lie down on the bed so they could finally shift me to the theater room. I was all prepped for the procedure. My heart felt so heavy. I didn't want to end this pregnancy, and I was all alone. I started crying hysterically. The doctors gave me anesthesia, and I was unconscious in seconds.

When I woke up, I felt miserable. I was no longer pregnant. I had no one with me except for my boyfriend's sister. I wanted him to be with me while I went through this terrible phase of my life. I kept thinking about the baby all the time. I knew what I did was wrong, but I had no choice. I was completely broken after the abortion. I felt worthless. After some time, the doctors came in again to check on me. She discharged me after making sure everything was okay.

His sister took me back to my boyfriend's house. He was still living with his parents. I remember I was not even able to look him in the eyes. I hated myself for what I did; I hated him for what he made me do. I was still feeling weak and vulnerable.

I wished he would show up at the clinic. I wanted him to be there, to support and care for me. Instead, he was supposed to drop me back at my house. We got into his car, and we hardly spoke. I did not know how to express my pain. On the whole way, none of us spoke a word. We were quiet the entire time. I was buried deep in my thoughts; I didn't even care if he was not talking to me.

He pulled over outside my house. As I was about to open the car's door to step out, he suddenly started crying. He didn't say a word, but he couldn't stop sobbing. I couldn't help myself, and I started crying too. We both cried but didn't say a word to each other. This was the first time that I had seen him cry. For some women, aborting a baby might be the most difficult decision; at least it was for me. I have always pictured myself with a big family and a loving husband. I wanted to have children, and when I did, I had to terminate it. I felt miserable and worthless even after years of my abortion. I would think about it all the time.

I thought, what had happened if I didn't do it?

What if I went along with my pregnancy?

I had no answers; no one did. It was a secret pregnancy and a secret abortion. No one knew what I went through except his parents. I believed they knew because I went back to his house after the abortion, and he was there with me. Nothing was said, but I was all alone, miserable, and depressed. But, going through all of that, I realised that no matter what, life goes on.

All of the things and the pain that you are going through, which you think will never leave you - will eventually go away. Time heals all the pain.

# Chapter 10
# The 10-year-long Depressive Episode

Sometimes, guilt is difficult to pin down. Thinking about your past can sometimes make your guilt sour, and that's when you become anxious and start to feel depressed all the time. No matter what situation you are in, your guilt can be a terrible burden.

You will become sensitive to your every action and have low self-esteem. There are precisely no words on how you can describe what a person is going through. But let me tell you, excessive guilt can make you suffer more than you think.

I was guilty - guilty of aborting my child. And that guilt overpowered me so much that it made me depressed for many years. I would grieve and think about the baby all the time, to the point where I started to lose interest in everything. My guilt and depression took a serious toll on my mental health.

After I broke up with my boyfriend and was alone for a few months. Then, I met another guy. We started talking as friends first and then developed a deeper relationship. As time passed, we became more serious with each other. It was my second serious relationship. We had our ups and downs, like many other couples, but we always worked through them.

On Christmas day, he proposed to me, which took me by surprise. We were finally engaged. Things were going well between us; we would go on dinner dates and sometimes watch a movie in the cinema. I loved him, and so did he; we were happy together.

There were times when we would argue or get in a fight occasionally, but it was for the time being. Then, one day, out of nowhere, he called me and said he wanted to end things with me. That took me by surprise as well; I was not expecting him to break up with me. I tried to talk to him when he told me that he was leaving me.

I wanted to sort things out, but he was adamant.

I cried a lot after our breakup. I took off my engagement ring and threw it on the ground out of frustration. I was already battling depression, and our breakup gave me much more to think about. So I was even more depressed after it.

Not long after, he came back and apologised for breaking up with me. He said he wanted me back, and he would make things like they were again. I was not sure if I could trust him again; he left me without warning and any excuses. I was unsure whether I should get back with him or not, but he eventually sweet-talked me into it.

Even though I agreed to be with him again and start a relationship, I told him I would not wear my engagement ring. After he had broken up with me, it had been hard for me to even look at my ring, and I didn't have the courage to wear it again. So, I told him that he would have to propose to me again. I wouldn't put that ring again on my finger.

But he was okay with that. Life was good again. We were back together, and we were happy.

One day, we weren't together, and I was lying in my bed, scrolling through my Facebook, when I saw that his relationship status had changed. I was surprised at this and did not know what to do.

I was heartbroken. I had trusted him even after all he had done to me. I couldn't believe my eyes when I saw that his Facebook relationship status had changed with someone else

I was devastated. My depression and anxiety made me do things I didn't expect to do. It messed up my head.

A month or so passed, and I was extremely depressed with everything going on in my life. I was unable to think or sleep properly. One day, out of the blue, he contacted me again and started apologising, just like he had done for the first time. He told me that leaving me was a mistake, and he was ashamed and guilty about it.

I didn't know what to do. I just listened to him apologising over and over again. Finally, he promised me he would not do anything stupid this time.

I agreed to be with him again.

We were back together, and things started to get back to normal. But I was battling my depression even more now. From the outside, I looked fine. But the depression was making me weak from the inside.

There were days when I couldn't keep anything down; I lost my appetite. I became so sensitive that even the smallest thing would trigger me, and I would start crying.

We went to Clacton for the holidays, where we had an amazing time. Then, one night, when we were out at a hotel, he proposed to me. I said 'Yes' in an instant. I was sure that we would always be happy together. I loved him, and I was ready to spend the rest of my life with him.

On the other hand, my depression was increasing. I started having frequent mood swings. I would find myself always upset and irritated. I also started experiencing insomnia; no matter what I did, I couldn't sleep.

When all of these symptoms persisted, I decided to get myself checked by my General Practitioner. So I went there and told him about all my symptoms. I mentioned everything, including what I felt, and he prescribed me a dose of antidepressants. He informed me that I had severe depression and should start taking those medications to feel better.

I came home and took a tablet as prescribed, hoping that I could start feeling better. But what I felt was the opposite of what I thought. I felt weird at first. Then, after some time, I started to feel nauseous, and I had a bad headache. Finally, my mouth went dry, and I felt sick.

I grabbed the box of those pills and threw them away in the trash can. Antidepressants did nothing for me. They made me feel even sicker, and I wouldn't say I liked it. I expected the medication to work in my favour, but it made me feel sicker. So, I continued to fight depression without any pills.

There was this one time when my ex-fiancé and I got into a pretty big fight. We were out somewhere when it happened, and we argued with each other the entire way in the car as well. I lived with my father at that time, so I asked him to drop me home as I couldn't take those arguments anymore. I was exhausted and tired from all the fighting.

He dropped me at the door and went straight off. I watched him as he left, but I didn't go inside the house. Instead, I walked to Highams Park. I was so angry at him and the situation that I couldn't help myself and started crying. I needed to talk to someone, and I felt like my head would explode out of frustration.

I took my phone out of my bag and called up a friend. I cried hysterically over the phone as I told him everything that had happened between me and my ex-fiancé. He was constantly trying to calm me down to stop crying, but I was so exhausted that I couldn't help it.

He kept asking me to go home and get some rest, but I couldn't. I wanted someone to come, snatch me and take me away. I wanted to run away from all my problems. Finally, my friend asked me to call him to sort things out. So, I hung up the phone.

I called my ex-fiancé and started yelling and arguing again. He sensed that I was not at home and somewhere else. I cried and yelled at him until he found me walking. He took me home again, and I received nothing from him. I figured out that my anxiety episodes were getting out of hand now, and I should do something about it. I was done being tired, anxious, and on edge all the time. So, I made a counselling session at Waltham Forest.

I had a few sessions at Waltham Forest. I talked with the professionals face to face, and it felt nice. I talked through everything, from what was happening in my life. I talked about my past, my guilt, and all of the things happening to me. I told the counsellor that I was done being depressed and I wanted to live a normal life.

The counsellor listened to everything I had to say, but he said he was still trying to figure me out. I was pretty bummed out when he said this; it made me feel that there was actually something wrong with me. He put my name down to see a physiatrist, and I was on the waiting list.

There are so many people who are struggling with mental illness. Everyone has their own set of problems that they deal with every day. Everyone looks so normal and calm from the outside, but we can never figure out what is happening inside their heads.

I realised it when I had to wait for months just to see a physiatrist. It is a healthy reminder always to be kind to people; you never know what they are going through.

One day, I went to Tesco to get some stuff that I needed. I remember I was in the Tesco car parking lot and ready to head home when my phone started to ring. I picked up my phone, and it was for my counselling session with the physiatrist. The person on the other side of the phone asked me a bunch of questions regarding my mental health.

I had a long conversation with the physiatrist over the phone while I was in the car parking area. The physiatrist asked me everything from the start and asked me how I was doing nowadays. Finally, she asked me if I wanted to get ahead with the treatment.

I declined in an instant.

I thought there was nothing wrong with me and that I would feel better with time. I have seen people getting better and better as time passes, and I thought I would be okay. Another reason for me to decline the treatment was because I was scared. Going to the counselling session and talking about my problems always made me anxious and resulted in me getting stressed out.

My ex-fiancé and I made some amazing memories in the time that we were together. He was there for me whenever I needed him. We went to a Taylor Swift concert; she was one of my favourite singers at that time. I used to listen to her songs all the time.

I even memorised her songs and would hum them all the time. He would also take me out to dinner and brunch dates in fancy restaurants. I loved him. He was there for me during all of my surgeries, supporting me and taking care of me.

I was still dealing with depression, and it would get worse sometimes, but my ex-fiancé was always there to calm me down. Of course, we still had our ups and downs, just like any normal couple, but I knew I wanted to spend the rest of my life with him until changes became confusing from living together.

# Chapter 11
# Wanting More

Ending a relationship is never easy, and it can be harder if it is a long-term relationship. You will feel sad, angry, frustrated, and depressed, and sometimes, these feelings can be very intense. You will keep thinking of what you did wrong, and that thought will kill you from the inside.

You will feel lonely and sad. But it's okay. It's okay to express your anger and pain. It is completely okay if your breakup hurts you more than you thought it would. Letting go of your emotions and thoughts is healthy for you. Don't complicate your life more with unnecessary *"what ifs," "maybe's,"* and *"if only's."* There will come a time when you will be at peace with yourself. You will be proud of yourself for overpowering a situation you thought would destroy you.

Things were going so well between me and my ex-fiancé. We were having the best time of our lives. I loved that he was always there for me whenever I needed support. He would make me laugh, care for me, and do everything that made me fall in love with him even more.

One day, we decided to move in together. I was still living

with my father at that time, so it was a huge step for me. After nine years of being together, it felt like I was getting closer to my dream; to get married and start a beautiful family. So, we started looking for a house. I was so excited when we started to look for our house. After looking for some weeks, we finally found a house that we both loved. My father also helped us get it; he was the one who put the deposit down.

It was a newly built home, and so it was very modern and stylish. It was a four-bedroom townhouse. We were only two people, but because I always wanted a big family, I wanted to get a big house, and I was ecstatic when we found the perfect one. My ex-fiancé and I moved in a few weeks later.

We both were so happy. Living together was new for both of us, and it had its own charms. We shopped for new furniture and started decorating the house the way we wanted. I also got some stuff for the baby and put it in the baby's room, even though we were not planning on starting a family at that time. But I always imagined my life having a big family, and I couldn't wait.

We would cook together, sing our favourite songs, and spend all of our time together. Life seemed like a fairy tale. We were both working; his workplace was just around the corner from our house. I had to travel miles away every day to go to my workplace. I made a decision to leave and started another job closer to home.

Time passed by, and I felt like we should move forward and get married. I couldn't wait to get married to the person I loved and start a family with him. So I talked to him about what I was feeling and what I wanted to do next. The first few times when I brought this topic up, he would brush it away, telling me that he would think about it. Months passed by, but he never said a word about us getting married. It felt like he was not ready to commit.

I grew more and more impatient as time passed by. I wanted to get married and have a baby, but my ex-fiancé did not show any interest in it. He would get irritated whenever I talked to him about our future. We had been in a relationship for almost nine years at that point and engaged. I wanted to start a family with him as it has always been my dream. However, there were times when he wouldn't even talk back when I asked him about our marriage or a baby. He kept me waiting.

I was so confused by his actions and behaviour. When a couple is engaged, the next thing is marriage and a family. But with us, things were different. I could see that he had no plans of marrying me or starting a family. I was already struggling with depression, and his behaviour gave me more to think about.

After spending so much time together, I started to feel like things were changing now. His actions made me think that he was uninterested in our future. I started having more depressive episodes, where I would lay in bed all day and think about our life together.

My ex-fiancé started to ignore me; even when he was at home, he would not talk to me and would stay busy doing his own stuff. He also started going out at really odd hours. I found myself alone in the big house where we were supposed to live happily together. I would sit there and wait for him to come home all day long. My depression soared.

I distinctly remember making plans for us to have a day outside, but he cancelled it all by telling me that he was busy that day. It felt like I was the only one fighting for our relationship. We also started to argue a lot. There was not a day that went by without us having a big fight.

Finally, he stopped compromising on things, like which furniture we should get for our room and other petty things. I missed the happy times that we had together. He became so aggressive and irritated, and I had no idea why. I wanted to fix things between us so we could go back to being a happy couple again, but I had no idea where to start.

One day, he started arguing with me over a tiny matter. I was already frustrated that day because of our constant fights over nothing. I said something, and he started yelling at me. I don't know how it happened, but our fight grew bigger. Then, out of nowhere, he grabbed me by my collar and dragged me along the bed, and I fell to the floor. I wasn't expecting this. I was crying, and he walked away. I hurt my left arm from how I landed. He came back into our bedroom, and I heard his footsteps. I was still sitting on the carpet floor, sobbing. He lent down to pick me up, but I shouted at him not to touch me and slapped him around the cheek of his face. Then he grabbed me and held me to the floor in our bedroom. I will never forget the look on his face. I did not know what was going to happen to me. I was crying, and the words coming out of his mouth were, "You're lucky I haven't killed you." and then he walked away.

It felt like the world stopped revolving around me. I stood still there, trying to wrap my head around what just happened. He physically abused me over a petty argument. We had been together for ten years now, and this was the first time that he had laid a hand on me. We had been into big fights before when we both yelled at each other, but physical abuse was never in the picture. I was numb. That was the worst day of my life. I still get goosebumps whenever I think about that day.

If you are in an abusive relationship, I sincerely advise you to step out of it as soon as possible. You may think that everything will fall in place eventually, and it is just a phase; no, it is not. It will only get worse with time. If you can get out of the relationship safely, do it before they hurt you again. Physically abusing your partner is never correct, no matter what the situation is. It is illegal, and you should take action against it right there.

I should have called the police right then and there, but I didn't. I loved him. I thought he did it because of stress, or maybe he was dealing with some work problems and didn't mean to hurt me; how could he? Time passed, and I moved on, hoping for the best. I thought things would change now, and he would realise what he did was wrong, but I was mistaken.

It was a normal day. My ex-fiancé came back home from work. He looked upset and confused. He entered the house and said, "I need to talk to you." I knew something was not right. We sat down, and I asked him what it was about.

He said, "Kaylie, I care about you, and I love you, but… I am not in love with you."

Before I could speak, he continued, "I don't want to be with you anymore. We should end this relationship."

I was still trying to process what he said to me. I knew something was off from the moment he came inside the house, but not in my wildest dreams had I thought he would break up with me that day. I had no words, and I started crying. I cried so much. I asked him why he was doing it and where I went wrong. I pleaded with him if he was mad at me over something, but he had no answer to any of my questions.

It was the third time that he was breaking up with me. I was always there for him, but he always did the opposite to me. He left me when I was in a vulnerable position in my life. I was angry and heartbroken. The person that I loved and trusted the most broke my heart into a million pieces. When he started acting weird the first time, I suspected that there was someone else. And now I was sure about it. I was sure that he was leaving me because he had found another girl. He went to stay at his parents' house, as he told me. My friends and family supported me through what seemed to be the hardest time of my life. Some days I felt like someone had drained all the life and energy out of me and had pushed me on a path that I wasn't prepared for.

Yet, my family and friends were always there for me, cheering me up and giving me positive hopes about my future. They made me understand that my life didn't end there, and I had so much to achieve. It was only because of them that I coped up with the situation better. I would be lost without the support of my family and friends.

I was left alone in the house where my ex-fiancé and I were supposed to start our life together. The empty house haunted me. The house that we got was bought under both of our names, and so it belonged to both of us. After a week or so, it's a difficult situation when the house belongs half and half. I had no choice but to not live here. He had rights. We had to live there until the house gets sold.

We tried to live civil in the house, but it was a disaster. We would be arguing and fighting every single day over everything. But we had to stay in the same house according to the laws, and we both couldn't leave.

I loved that house. I never wanted to sell it in the first place, but I had to. I could not afford such a big and expensive house on my own at that time, so I was left with no choice but to sell it. It seemed like I was moving further away from my dream of starting a family.

My life and my mind were in chaos. I had no idea what I would do in the future. I was depressed and heartbroken, and it felt like everything was crumbling up in front of my eyes.

It took me quite some time to get over my ex-fiancé. It took me a while to let go of my emotions. Finally, I realised that my life was very much here; he was just a person that left. I continued to work for my dreams, and I am glad that I did.

# Chapter 12
# The Final Relationship

Ending a relationship is complicated and stressful. Breaking up with the person you love will make you feel emotionally drained and heartbroken; there is no way around it.

Lost relationships deserve to be grieved over. But, no matter who ended it, there is a loss of hopes and dreams that needs to be faced. You will be awake all night, trying to process what went wrong. You will be in the middle of crying fits while battling anxiety and depression, and you will feel like it is impossible to survive without that person.

But, the good news is, when you get over it, you will feel free of all the toxicity. You will be ready to meet someone who will be a better match for you and someone who will treat you like you deserve. So, it is completely okay for you to take some time to grieve the loss of a relationship. But don't wallow in that emotion; know that there will be brighter days ahead, and you will be happy again.

I grieved too. I cried most of the nights and slept all day long. I was a mess; I was not able to cope with what happened. Because we had been together for so long, it was harder for me to accept that it was all over. There were days when I felt like I was okay and ready to move on, but then I would find myself crying for him all over again the next day.

I was very depressed during those few weeks.

After weeks of crying and mourning, I thought it was time for me to move on. I could not keep crying for someone who treated me the way he had. I had my whole life ahead of me, and I wanted to live it to the fullest. I wanted to put myself out to the world again and search for my Mr. Right.

I started scrolling through my social media and dating apps. Finally, I met a guy online. He was friendly and respectful. I slowly started to regain my confidence. After talking for a couple of days, we decided to meet in person. We had a good time together; we held hands and kissed as we ended the night.

I waited for him to text or call me back, but he didn't do that for two days. Finally, the next day, I received a call from him.

"I am not looking for a serious relationship," he said as soon as I picked up the call.

There was nothing more to say. I was distraught. I thought I would never find someone for me. Negative thoughts started creeping into my mind once again until I met another guy some days after. I am, still to this day, with the second guy I met online.

His name is Jason. It was October 2019 when we met for the first time. Initially, we talked over messages for the first time, and it felt like we instantly clicked with each other. I was having a great time just talking to him like this.

I remember the first time when we talked over the phone. I felt a thousand butterflies in my stomach when I heard his voice. I loved his voice. After talking over the phone through messages and calls, we thought it was time to meet in person. So we decided to meet at TGIF, which is a restaurant based in Braintree, Essex.

On the day we were supposed to meet, I was very nervous. I really liked Jason and didn't want anything to go wrong. I have always heard that *the first impression is the last impression,* so I wanted to make a good impression the first time we met.

I had seen Jason in some of the pictures that he sent. But, meeting in person is different. It is hard to meet someone for the first time in a crowded place. I pulled my car into the parking lot and called my mother to tell her that I had arrived. I was constantly scanning the crowd, trying to spot Jason and my eyes were fixed on a guy standing out among the crowd.

"That is him!" I said to my mother, who was still on the phone with me.

"How do you know?" My mother asked me.

"Because it seems like he is waiting for someone. I'll call you back," I told her and hung up the phone.

I looked in the mirror one last time and got out of my car. I went up the stairs and straight towards where the guy was standing. As I got close enough, I asked, "Jason?"

"Kaylie?" he said, and we both smiled.

We went inside the restaurant and sat down. We got to talking about different things; I was having a nice time with Jason. I ordered the Jack Daniels Chicken; I was surprised when Jason placed his order. He ordered ribs.

*"Ribs on the first date? He is going to make a mess!"* I thought to myself.

Surprisingly, he didn't make a mess. Instead, he ate very carefully, and he used a fork and a knife to eat his food.

Jason and I couldn't stop talking. We had so much to talk about; it didn't feel like we were meeting for the first time. We took turns in asking questions. He would ask a question, and I answered it. Then it was my turn to ask a question, and he would answer it. We got to know a lot about each other this way. Jason and I were both very honest with our answers.

Our questions got more serious with time. I asked what he wanted in life, and I couldn't believe it when he said he wanted marriage, a family, and a home. These were the things that I have always wanted from the start.

I started to like him more and more after his opinions on life. He was cute, and we had a fantastic time with each other. We were so into each other that we didn't even realise that the restaurant was closing. We got up from there and sat in my car for a bit longer. I also told him about the situation with my ex-fiancé.

I told him about my disability in the car. I was nervous to tell him about it. I really liked Jason, and I didn't want things to end between us. It took me a while to tell him everything about myself. When I told Jason, he went silent for a while. It looked like he was trying to process what I had told him.

"Why didn't you tell me?" Jason asked after a while.

I was relieved that he said something. I told him that I thought he wouldn't like me after I told him about my disability. Jason told me that he liked me and cared for me. He also told me that he doesn't care about my disabilities. We talked a bit longer and said our goodbyes. He went home, and I came to my place. After some time, Jason asked me out on another date, and of course, I said yes.

"Dress smart!" Jason said over the call.

I had no idea what he was planning. It was the day of our second date. I was almost ready when the doorbell rang. I answered the door and found Jason standing there. He was wearing a navy blue suit, and he had a beautiful bouquet of roses in his hand. I loved this gesture so much. I asked him to come inside. I put the roses in a vase and took them up to my room.

That day, I was also wearing a navy blue dress, and I realised that we were matching, coincidentally. So, I had to grab my shoes, and I was all ready for our date.

"Sorry, I don't have a limo," Jason said as I was putting my shoes on.

"It's okay!" I replied in an instant.

Jason picked me up in his van. Then, we got in his car and went off. On the way, I asked Jason where we were going; he said it was a surprise. But, I had guessed already what he was trying to do. When we were on our first date, Jason asked me what my ideal date would be, and I told him that I would love for someone to pick me up from my house in a limo, give me red roses and have dinner in a fancy restaurant. That was what Jason was doing, and I loved it.

He took me to a fancy restaurant, just the way I wanted my perfect date to be. It didn't feel real. I tried to be careful on our second date and not clumsy. I didn't want anything to go wrong on our perfect date. It was an amazing night for Jason and me. He talked, held hands, and when it was time to say goodnight, we kissed.

After dating for some time, Jason asked me to come with him to a cottage and meet his parents. So, we stayed at the cottage with his parents for a few days. I loved Jason's parents. They were so sweet, and I adored them like my own parents.

We had a wonderful time at the cottage. Living with Jason at the cottage made me fall for him. When we started dating, I didn't know if this relationship would work or how love was supposed to feel. But he somehow made me fall for him. He cared about me, respected me, and loved me all the time.

One night at the cottage, Jason and I were sitting together. We were looking into each other's eyes, and that was the first time we confessed our love to each other. Jason was about to say "I love you" to me, but I beat him to it and said it first. He told me that he loved me too. That night was like a fairytale, and it was perfect in every way.

Being with Jason at the cottage was beautiful. I forgot all of my worries there. I felt like my life was perfect with Jason, and I wanted nothing more. But, I forgot about my ex, who was still living with me back home. So, when it was time to go back, I started to feel anxious.

I didn't want to see his face again after spending those wonderful days with Jason. My ex had made my life miserable. He would fight and argue with me all the time. It felt like I was going back into a hellhole again.

When I went back home, all the fighting and the arguing started again. My ex told me that he was seeing someone, and it did not surprise me. I knew there was a reason for him leaving me and that it was another girl. But at that point, I didn't care.

I had Jason, and I was in love with him. But, sometimes, my ex would frustrate me so much that I wanted to run away and leave the house. I even called Jason twice, crying. Finally, I told him that it was now impossible for me to live under the same roof as my ex.

Jason asked me to come to his place. As soon as I got to his house, he hugged me tightly and didn't let me go for a few minutes. I felt like Jason was my protector. I felt safe around him. That day, Jason gave me spare keys to his house and told me that I could come to his place whenever I wanted.

His gesture made me so happy, and it made me fall in love with him even more.

As days passed by, my ex started to irritate me even more. He made my life miserable. I loved my house, and I wanted to live there alone, but I was left with no choice again. Finally, Jason and I decided that I should move in with him, so I did just that. I moved in after a few days. I was relieved. Jason and I loved being with each other; we were happy with each other's presence. I was happy that I didn't have to see my ex's face every day.

My ex didn't leave me then; he would call me all the time and message me regarding the house. Then, whenever we decided to meet and talk about the process of the house, he would argue with me, and he would try to control me in following his steps.

Even after moving out, my ex did his best to make my life miserable. But I had Jason; he would calm me down and listen to my rants. Jason was the best thing in my life at that time when everything was uncertain. He deeply cared for me, and I did for him.

After I broke up with my ex, I never thought I would find love again, but I did. Breaking up with my ex and finding Jason made me realise that there is so much out there that the world has to offer. We just have to search for our light even when we think there is only darkness for us.

# Chapter 13
# Reunited After 18 Years

The relationship of siblings is one of the strongest relationships in the world. Siblings impact your life in many ways. They are a child's first playmate and an adult's trusted friend.

The connection between siblings is hard to describe in a word. It is more of a feeling that you have towards each other. Even if you didn't talk to your brother or sister for some time, you know they are there for you, and they have got your back. The relationship of siblings is amazing; it's the bond that you share with each other. It's the fact that you pick up right where you left off, even if it has been months since you last met each other.

I grew up with my sister. We lived with our father, and we had the best time together. Over the weekends, when we visited our mother, we would have our girls' moments and enjoy life to its fullest. My sister and I always shared a good bond. We were there for each other from the start. We would play together, sing together, and study together as well. I was grateful for the bond that my sister and I shared. She was my first friend and a great advisor.

I also had a brother, Reece. He was my half-brother from my mother's previous boyfriend. Before my sister and I moved to my father's house, I had met him. I met him since he was born. But I hardly saw him when I was in the hospital. My mother stated he was with his father and family while she stayed at the hospital with me. I remembered him even when I grew up, and I missed him. So, when I hit my teens, I started searching for him.

I was told multiple stories by many people about my half-brother. Some would tell me that he lives with his father, and some would tell me a completely different story. I didn't want to be a part of all that mess; I just wanted my half-brother to be a part of my life. So, I asked my mother for help.

She gave me his father's contact number. I remember, after I got the number, I called him while I was sitting in my car. I was shocked to hear his reply when I told him who I was. He said he didn't know me or my sister. I talked to him some more because I really wanted to talk to my half-brother. My mother's ex told me that it was not a good time as my half-brother was giving his GSCE's. He also said that he would try and talk to Reece to add me on Facebook so we could get in contact. He did not tell me anything more than that, so I gave up and hung up the phone.

I knew my half-brother's full name, so I would search him on Facebook every now and then, but I had no luck. He never appeared on my search feed until, one day, he did. There was a time when I almost gave up looking for him because there were so many people who had identical names, and I hadn't seen him in the last eighteen years, so I had no idea how he looked. I was so happy and thrilled the day when I found my brother.

Without wasting any time, I sent him a friend request on Facebook and privately messaged him, saying, "hi." That was how Reece and I started talking.

Social media is such a powerful tool in this era. Sometimes when I think about it, it amazes me. Social media gives you the power to do anything that you want. You can easily find your missing friends, the ones you lost contact with when you graduated from school. I found my lost brother through social media, and I am thankful for it. I would have never been able to find him without searching him up. So, I thank the internet entirely for that.

I was talking to Reece after eighteen long years. It felt surreal. I saw him last when he was just a baby, and we were adults now. When we started talking, I felt a natural instant connection with him. When we first started talking, we would chat and speak from time to time. I told my half-brother that I didn't want to know anything about the past; I just wanted us to have a good brother-sister relationship now. We also started talking on the phone. I would call him when I was free, and sometimes, he would call me, and we would talk about everything. We never talked about what happened in the past. For me, there was nothing we both could do about the past now. It was all long gone. I also tried to stay out of all the messed-up family matters, so I had no information or proof of what happened.

My brother and I started to send gifts and cards at events like birthdays or Christmas. It felt so good to be in contact with him again. After some time of talking over messages and calls, we decided to meet each other finally. We planned everything, but something came up every time, and we were unable to meet. We planned our meet-up when I was with my ex-fiancé. I told him that my fiancé would also be there, but he refused. I realised that I was very nervous about meeting him alone, and I wanted someone else's support to meet my brother. We would always plan to meet up after that, but something or the other would come up, and we were never able to meet each other.

After that, we decided that he would come over to my place. So, I met my half-brother, Reece, in 2020; he came over to my house as we had decided. It was after I got engaged with Jason. I asked him if it was okay for him to meet my fiancé, Jason, for the first time. He said he didn't mind, and I was excited about him meeting Jason, just like I was excited about meeting my brother.

It was finally the day when my brother was coming to meet me. I was so excited that day. Finally, I met him after eighteen years. Jason was not at home when I heard the knocking on the door. I knew it was him because Jason had the keys, so he never knocked. My heart started pounding, and I didn't know what to expect. I hadn't seen him since he was a 2-year-old boy.

I was nervous and excited at the same time. I looked through the peephole and realised it was him standing outside the door. I opened the door, and we smiled at each other. We hugged each other for a while, which felt like ages. I couldn't believe it was my brother standing at the door.

Just by looking at him, I could tell that he resembled me and my sister very much. He had the face of my sister, and his eyes were just like mine. I never knew we would get along so well. We instantly clicked, and I loved his company.

I had a feeling that our first meeting would be a little awkward as we would see each other after ages. I thought we wouldn't have anything to talk about, and we would sit there awkwardly in silence. But to my surprise, meeting him for the first time was not even close to being awkward. It didn't feel like we were seeing each other for the first time.

We talked about everything openly. We laughed and enjoyed our time together. Meeting my half-brother felt like a piece of the puzzle was missing for the longest time, and he was that missing puzzle piece. He fit right in.

After a while of us talking, Jason came home. I really

wanted Jason and my brother to get along well. I didn't want to lose anyone of them; they were both important people in my life. So, I was happy to see Jason and my brother getting along well; they talked and enjoyed each other's company. I took a sigh of relief as I watched them.

We went to a restaurant for dinner, and the atmosphere was lovely. I noticed that my brother was very protective of me. He told Jason to take good care of me, as he knew that things had gotten bad with my ex. I always wanted a brother who would defend me and take care of me, and I finally got that brother. He told me that he was tipsy and that he was having a really good time with me and Jason.

We went home after having a lovely dinner. I put on some light music in the background while we played cards. Jason, Reece, and I laughed at the silliest things, and we had an amazing time together. Reece also asked if he could stay at our place because it got late that day. I was excited for him to stay with us, so we said yes.

Even to this day, we meet each other. My brother is an important part of my life now, and I cherish him for that.

# Chapter 14
# Cutting Off

Mental illness is as real as cancer or a broken leg. It can be diagnosed and treated with the same certainty as any other disease.

But unfortunately, there are so many people out there who still believe that mental illness is a weakness of character, a mere confusion, or just a flaw.

Many people who are struggling with mental health problems don't get treatment. Either they have no idea what they are dealing with, or they are held back by the social stigma of mental illness. Unfortunately, this stops them from getting the treatment they need to feel better.

Any mental illness, if not treated on time, can worsen quickly. In some cases, untreated mental illness can also lead a person to end their own life. Mental health is real, and anyone who is showing signs of it should take it seriously, just as any other medical problem. You would get your broken leg fixed, right?

After all of the things that I had been through, I started experiencing depressive episodes. It all started when I was dating my ex-fiancé. Even though he was not supportive of my mental illness, I knew I was not fine. There were days when I would cry for no reason at all. I lost my appetite to the point where even looking at food would make me puke, and I refused treatment as well.

Experiencing mental illness and struggling with depression and anxiety is one of the worst things people can go through. You never know how the person in front of you is going to react; they can be very supportive of the things that you are going through, or they can just sit there and watch you like you are faking it.

Going through the break-up with my ex was hard, and it took a huge toll on my mental health. I was already battling depression, mental issues, and the break-up, and his constant nagging was a cherry on top. Even though Jason was there for me and he knew all about my mental conditions, there were days when I wanted to be left alone. Here is another worst thing that people with mental illness go through; they want to be alone, even when people are supporting them.

After I moved in with Jason, things slowly started getting better. I felt relaxed, loved, and comforted every day, which was rare when living civil with my ex. Instead, he made my life miserable, and he played a massive part in making my mental health worse than it already was. I still felt sad and unhappy, even when Jason was there for me. That was when I realised that these were not just phases and that my mental health was declining day by day.

Depression made things turn so ugly for me that it started to take a toll on my daily activities. I lost interest in everything that I loved to do. I wanted to sit on the couch all day in my pyjamas. I wanted to be left alone, and I would be unhappy and usually in a bad mood all the time. I lost interest in my job. And suddenly, waking up in the mornings became the hardest for me.

I couldn't get myself together to get out of bed and change into some decent clothes. It was too much work for me. It all came to a point where I didn't even care about my work. As a result, I lost my job.

I felt like I couldn't cope with anything, from work to simple house chores like doing the dishes. I felt sick all the time, even when I wasn't. I would feel nauseous, weak, and sick to my stomach. Food was not really my friend when I was fighting depression. I ate very little throughout the day, and I was always lying down somewhere in the house, unable to get up and get some work done.

Finally, I realised that I should never have stopped my treatment, which I refused and stopped years ago. When I first experienced depression, I went to counselling. Even though going there helped me, I never continued my treatment to see a physiatrist. Refusing treatment for my mental health was the biggest mistake that I made years back, and I was now paying for the consequences.

My ex was not supportive at all. He was never really there for me; even when I was severely depressed, it felt like he didn't care. Jason was the complete opposite of my ex, and I was so happy that I met him. He was always there for me when I was at my worst. Jason would try his best to comfort me and bring me back to normal. Unfortunately, my condition kept getting worse every day.

After some time of battling with mental issues, I started experiencing heart palpitations. I felt like my heart was always running a marathon. I would get out of breath even when I was sitting or lying on the bed. There were some days when I felt like I couldn't breathe properly.

When my mental illness started to show itself physically, I knew it was time to see a physiatrist. I started experiencing body weakness and increased heart rate, but I didn't know how. After I declined my treatment the first time, I was unsure of going with worsening conditions.

Jason encouraged me that I should get in touch with my GP because my condition was getting out of hand. He was there for me, and I loved it about him. Jason always showed his care and affection towards me differently, and I was grateful for a person like him. He was the opposite of my ex. On the contrary, he always supported me and believed in me. So Jason and I decided to go together to my GP.

I went there with Jason and told her all about my condition. I told her about the depressive episodes and how I could not get up and do simple tasks, like brushing my hair or drinking a glass of water. I also told my general practitioner how my heart rate was always higher, and I felt like I couldn't breathe. I told my doctor everything in detail; my GP confirmed that I was experiencing severe depression and anxiety. It totally got worse over the years, and it was now taking over my physical health as well.

My GP prescribed me some medications for my depression and anxiety. She also gave me some medicines to help with my heart palpitations. I thought I would feel better once I visited a doctor, but I was wrong. I didn't feel better even in the slightest. I was also not sure about the medications that he prescribed for me.

There were a hundred questions and a thousand what-ifs in my mind about the medicines. I think it was because of the mental illness that I imagined the worst outcomes possible. Just by looking at all those colourful pills, I thought something would go horribly wrong once I started taking them.

After my doctor's appointment, Jason and I came back home. We had dinner together, and when it was time to take my pills, I hesitated. No matter what I did, I couldn't convince my mind to start the treatment. To this day, I am not too sure about those medications. I talked to Jason about how I was feeling, and he supported me there as well. Jason told me that he wanted me to get better without popping those pills.

Jason had seen some horrible cases of mental illness getting worse with medications, so he preferred if I didn't take those and get better with counselling. I sat there, still not sure how to take things further on. I was not sure if I should take the medicines that my doctor gave me. Talking with Jason about it helped me a lot. He told me that he would support me and be there for me no matter what.

Jason comforted me. I liked knowing that he got my back always. Because I had lost my job, Jason told me that he would pay for my counselling sessions if they were needed.

Whenever Jason told me that he was there for me, he would always find ways to show me that. It was his little gestures that made me fall for him. Jason knew how to comfort me, even when I was at my worst. I don't know how, but his words always soothed my raging anxiety, and I would feel somewhat better instantly.

Jason was so nice to me that sometimes, it felt like I was in a fairytale. Whenever I would feel just a little anxious or upset, he would make sure I felt better. What Jason did for me sometimes just didn't feel real. Maybe, it was because I had a terrible past where I would never find my ex anywhere for support. He made me feel bad for having mental issues, and that feeling made me even more conscious.

I realised how I should be treated, which I never did in my past relationships. I always felt at fault when I was with my ex because of my mental health. He would never miss a chance to make me feel worthless. So I felt bad for being sad and depressed. But with Jason, I realised I should have always been treated like that. Jason made me realise my worth. He made me understand that I was worthy of every good thing in the world, even when I didn't see it. And that is what he did; he made me see how worthy I am.

I was still battling extreme depression when one day, it all came crashing down on me. I was alone at home that day, and Jason was at work. I was distraught since I woke up that day; I didn't feel like eating anything or talking to anyone. That day was hard, and I just wanted to lay down in a corner somewhere and ignore the world.

When Jason left for work, it got worse. As the day passed, I started to feel more depressed. Then, for no reason at all, I started crying. I cried so much that day, and I didn't even know why I was crying. I don't know how, but the thought of overdosing with the same colourful pills hit my mind. The pain was so real and had walloped me that I saw overdosing as the only way out. But I guess I wasn't in my senses at that time.

I went over to the drawer and took out my GP's medications for my depression. I had no guts in myself, so I stared at the tablets while all of the negative thoughts clouded my mind.

I wanted to overdose myself so that I could get out of the constant pain. I popped all of the tablets out of their boxes and stared at them again. I don't even remember for how long I had those in my hands and for how long I was staring right at them. Just like that, I snapped out of my thoughts. I threw the tablets in the bin before I dared to overdose again.

Just as I threw the tablets in the bin, Jason came in and saw me. He looked at the terrible state I was in. He saw my tears and the worried look on my face. He came and sat next to me, and I told him everything. I told him about the suicidal thoughts that I had when I looked at the medications. Jason didn't say a word. Instead, he hugged me tightly. We sat there with each other for a while, and again, Jason brought comfort to me. I was glad that he came home. I felt safe when he was around.

I threw those medications away in the trash can. I feared even looking at them again. I dreaded the thought of overdosing, and I didn't want those horrible to come back ever again.

I'm unable to describe the state that I was in, and I felt unreal. The pain was so intense that it made me decide to end it myself. Mental illness is so real, even if no one sees it that way. It can cause chaos in your life, disturbing everything that you have. Depression can take a toll on your life and your mind. And before you know it, you will be taking steps unconsciously to end the pain somehow.

# Chapter 15
# Long-awaited Dream

*"Let the power of your love change the world, but never let the problems of this world change the beauty of your love."*

— Debasish Mridha

Love is the most beautiful feeling on earth. It is a feeling of attachment and affection. It is so strong that it can change our life upside down. It makes you hopeful.

Love makes you look at life differently, even if you are going through something terrible. Because you know that someone will be there for you when you get tired; there will be someone to hold you, motivate you, and their love will keep you going.

One day, I had to go back to my house. It was the house where my ex and I decided to move in together, the house in which we broke up and lived, civil. The same place I once called 'home.' I had a strange feeling since I decided to revisit my old place; maybe it was because I knew my ex was still there. And the thought of seeing him again and going back there, where I have had so many bad memories, haunted me.

I parked my car outside of the house, and I started crying

hysterically. My ex-fiancé and I bought it with so many dreams, and it was now time to let go. I was still crying when I unlocked the door and went inside. It was my dream home, and it was very hard for me to say goodbye because I didn't want to.

I looked around and sighed in relief when I found out my ex wasn't there. I could see that he had started packing his things and was ready to move out. I couldn't believe I had to let go of the house, but I had to. Yet again, I was forced to make a decision that I was not ready for. So, I just sat there and started sobbing uncontrollably. It was painful to be like this, and it got harder for me to control myself after a while. Ultimately, I was left with no other option than to call on a mental health helpline.

The person on the other side of the phone tried his best to calm me down. He asked me to take deep breaths and think about something positive, but nothing was helping. I couldn't stop crying, no matter what he said. Not being able to take it anymore, I hung up the phone and called Jason. He was nearby when I called him, and he came rushing to me. I felt better just hearing Jason say that he was coming to get me. Once again, he proved his love for me.

Jason came and stood by me when I needed him the most. He came inside and sat beside me. His presence was enough for me to feel that I wasn't alone and that someone was there for me.

Just after a few weeks of our relationship, I knew I had to get rid of the engagement ring that my ex had given me. It meant nothing to me anymore, and I thought it would make someone else's dream come true, if not mine. I got upset whenever I looked at it. It brought nothing but the painful and haunting memories of my past. And so, I decided to do away with the pain and sell the ring.

Even though I had no feelings for my ex or the ring, it was still hard for me to go alone and sell it. I asked Jason if he could come with me, and of course, he agreed. Jason and I went to the jeweler's, and he waited outside for me. It felt good to know that he was right there, supporting me no matter what.

I went into that store and sold the ring. It was painful for me to watch it go as I collected the cash. I was going through this all just because of my ex, I wanted our relationship, and I knew I did nothing wrong. But this was the state of things. I had to accept that nothing could be done.

As soon I stepped outside, I hugged Jason and started crying. I was overwhelmed with emotion, and it was so much for me to handle. But Jason held me tight, and I knew he was not going anywhere. It was all I needed to know at that time. The warmth and comfort that I got from him helped the pain become much more bearable.

In January 2020, Jason said something to me that was totally unexpected. We were talking, and suddenly, he said that he wanted a baby. I was happy but shocked because I didn't expect him to say it out loud.

I loved Jason. And saying what he did, made me feel the happiest I had felt in a long time. All my worries and sadness magically disappeared when he told me he wanted us to have a baby. All I wished for in my life was a happy family, and that day, it felt like my dreams were finally coming true.

I remember my ex saying that we would start a family only when he felt ready, which he never did. Instead, he kept me waiting for years even though he knew that was what I wanted in my life, a big happy family.

In February 2020, Jason and I decided to go on a vacation together. We only had a few days because of Jason's work responsibilities, but those were the best days of my life. We went on a mini-holiday to Costa Del Sol, Spain. I had never been on holiday alone with my boyfriend, so it was my first time with Jason. I was excited and happy that Jason wanted to spend his time with me at a magical place. The time that we spent together in Spain was amazing. I was wonderstruck by the place, and being there with the person I loved made it even more beautiful.

Every minute that Jason and I spent together was wonderful. It was amazing how one person could make all of your worries go away. We would go out for long strolls on the beach at night and lay by the pool in the morning. We drank cocktails, ate terrific food, and played cards together. I still remember how free and happy I felt in those days. Jason and I were the happiest there. We cared for each other and loved each other. We wanted nothing more.

Valentine's day was around the corner. It was the day when people showed their love and affection for the person they loved. So, of course, I expected Jason would do something special for me. But what he actually did meant so much more to me.

In my previous relationship, my ex gifted me a Pandora bracelet. I loved that bracelet, and I used to wear it all the time until we broke up. And just like that, the scars of the relationship found their way onto this gift. In one second, the bracelet I loved wearing became meaningless to me in a second, and I had no option rather than to throw it away.

After our breakup, I couldn't even look at that bracelet, and I was glad to get rid of it. So, on Valentine's Day, Jason gave me another Pandora bracelet to replace the one I had.

The bracelet that Jason gave me was so beautiful that I couldn't stop looking at it. It was one of the best presents that Jason gave me. Even though it was almost the same as the one I had before, it was a hundred times more valuable to me. Jason was always so thoughtful of everything that he did, and I loved it about him. He bought me a new bracelet to start my chapter with him, and I loved it. It was the best valentine's gift I could ask for.

Things were going great with Jason and me. We were happy together. I still had depressive episodes, but I knew things would get better one day. Being positive helped me cope with depression, and I started to look at the world differently.

One day, I woke up and felt a pinching pain in my legs. I didn't know what was happening. To this day, I remember the horrible pain that I dealt with when I was a child. I went through surgery after surgery to get better. But, I was scared to feel the same pain in my legs again.

I was already dealing with mental issues, and I knew I wouldn't be able to deal with more pain. As time passed, the pain started to get consistent. Some days were the worst when I would wake up with excruciating pain in my legs.

I was weak and lazy, and it felt like I had no energy left to do anything. My body ached whenever I tried lifting anything that was even slightly heavy. Weeks and months passed by, and my pain grew worse.

My mental health deteriorated as my leg pains grew worse. It was so much for me to handle, and I couldn't wait to start my treatment. So, In December 2020, I started my counselling sessions.

Jason was highly supportive of me through all of this. He knew how confused and nervous I was, and he tried his best to keep me motivated. Jason told me that he wanted me to get better to have the best time together. Imagining a future with him was all I wanted, and I was ready to do anything for him.

All it took were just a few sessions for me to start feeling better. I was amazed at how counselling was helping me recover. Finally, I started looking at life positively. All of the negative thoughts that I had started to disappear, and I couldn't have asked for more. Those thoughts were a disaster for me, they made me take my own life once, and I never wanted to experience such dark thoughts ever again.

Counselling also helped me forget my ex and all of the things that he did to me. My memories of my ex, the time we spent together, and all of our fights started fading away slowly, and I felt like I was coming back to life. There were times I felt I was seeing a ghost of him, standing by the doorway, watching me. I started to be happy, and that made Jason happy. The progress was slow, but it was there, and that was enough for me.

During all of the tough times, I am glad and grateful for Jason for standing right beside me, supporting and loving me every step of the way. Love truly is magical, and I realised it because of him.

# Chapter 16
# The Proposal

After you have been through so much in your life, sometimes it is okay not to be okay. There is nothing wrong with being scared. Everyone is different and needs time to move on with their life. Going through trauma or abuse is not easy; it shakes your soul and makes you feel weak and helpless.

Jason gave a new meaning to my dull and toxic life. He showed me how beautiful it is to be loved by someone, and he proved to be there for me every step of the way. I have been through a lot in my life, and since I met Jason, I have always found him supporting and pushing me through all of the chaos.

Jason and I would visit both our parent's houses frequently. I loved Jason's parents; they were the sweetest people I have ever met.

On 12th July 2020, we went to his parent's place in Bournemouth. It was my birthday, and we were getting ready to go out for my birthday dinner. I was facing the mirror when Jason knelt on one knee. I was confused at what was happening until he pulled out a ring from his pocket. That's when I knew he was going to propose.

## The Beautiful Survivor

I remember telling Jason on our very first date that I wanted to find my soul mate, get married, and start a beautiful family before I turned 30 years old. I laughed as those words escaped my mouth because I knew there was just a little time left for me to have all of my dreams come true. I had wasted so many years waiting for my ex-fiancé to get ready for marriage.

I couldn't believe it was happening and didn't expect him to propose so soon. It felt like I was dreaming, or even if I was, it would have been the best dream ever.

Jason stood behind me, and when I turned back, he was kneeling on one knee, holding the most beautiful ring I had ever seen in my life. He proposed to me in the best way possible. He told me that I was the love of his life and the first person that he loved. I instantly said yes, of course. I had been waiting for this very moment my entire life. It was my dream to get married to the person I love the most, and that night, Jason made it come to life.

When he proposed, I couldn't believe how soon it was. I kept thinking that he must have really loved me to do this and for being with me for a year even when my ex was still involved in our lives. He stood by me at my lowest and when I was struggling with extreme mental health issues. Jason was there for me; he knew how hard it was for me to get rid of my engagement ring.

Gently taking my hand in his, Jason slipped the ring onto

my finger. It was a white gold ring with a diamond that shone brightly at me. He even got *"forever"* engraved inside the belt of the ring.

I was so happy that I couldn't stop smiling. It was our happy moment, and I wanted to enjoy it as much as I could. After going through so much in my life, I got something that I truly wished for and dreamt of. Every moment was perfect, and I couldn't be happier. I kept thinking, *'what type of man would go through all this for one person? I'm just happy he is willing to show that he is 100% ready to marry me and start our lives together as husband and wife.'*

Jason and I went downstairs and told his parents the good news. To this day, I remember the happiness on their faces.

We went to a restaurant with Jason's parents for my birthday dinner. Jason's mother asked us if we had planned where we wanted to get married. I had already planned everything about my wedding years ago. Just when I was about to tell her the place that I thought would be perfect for our wedding, Jason beat me to it and told her about the same place. I couldn't believe he said Oxford Spires Hotel because that was what I had in mind. I was happy that we both wanted a big, beautiful wedding.

Things were amazing after we got engaged. We were the happiest couple, and I was over the moon. After that, life seemed different, happier, and peaceful. I updated my relationship status on social media the same night, and Jason and I were overwhelmed with the lovely comments that we received on the post.

Jason and I started to plan every little detail of our wedding from the same day. I could see how happy he was, and it was all I wanted.

It was September 2020 when I got a call that my house was finally getting sold. I was happy and relieved but sad at the same time. I remember how excited I was when I bought that house with my ex-fiancé. I thought it was my dream house, where I would start a family and live a happy life. But all of my dreams came crashing down just over a year after my ex and I moved in there.

I loved that house, and I never wanted to sell it. But I knew I didn't have any other option rather than to let it go. It just had to be done. All in all, it took about a year of me and my ex-fiancé splitting up for the house to finally get sold. It was an emotionally challenging year for me. If nothing else, I would now be able to get rid of the burden it had on me.

Even though I was not in contact with my ex-fiancé, I still felt like he was somehow part of my life. So when I received the call that the house was getting sold, I was relieved. I thought this was it. Now I could finally cut all the ties with my ex-fiancé after that. But I was wrong.

Although the house was gone, I was not able to get my ex-fiancé out of my head. The torture that he put me through was still there, and I couldn't get past that no matter what I did. No matter what, I wouldn't be able to regain that peace.

I would imagine the worst scenarios of him coming back after me. It was easy to get scared when you had been through a lot with someone who tortured you every single day, someone who made your life miserable. The fear never leaves you. And so, I was scared of being alone, even at my own house.

I used to have nightmares of him, and I would wake up with a jolt in the middle of the night. Sometimes, I would see his reflection whenever I was alone in the house. I now know that my mind played tricks on me. But at the time, I was convinced he was following me. A lot of the time, I would get scared, thinking that I had seen his ghost in my house. The thought of him coming after me was always there at the back of my mind, and it haunted me.

I knew it was a sign of fear. Seeing him like this, as a ghost, was nothing but a series of hallucinations. It was not easy for me to live in constant fear; it triggered anxiety badly at times.

My ex-fiancé had made my life miserable; he hurt me with his actions and caused me to live in pain. I thought I would move on after the house got sold, but I was still standing there. It was very difficult for me to move on, knowing what he did to my family and me. It was hard for me to come around to the fact that he went away freely even after what he did.

Jason knew how controlling and rude he was. He would be there with me whenever I talked to my ex-fiancé regarding the house. As Jason started noticing these conversations, he would tip me off about manipulative the behaviour looked. I had only been accustomed to my insider perspective, so I couldn't deny that he was right about it. My ex-fiancé used to talk to me in a repulsive manner. He thought I was his slave, and I was obliged to do everything he asked me to.

I lost my self-esteem when I was in my previous relationship. I was made to think that I was worthless and someone that could be used as a doormat or a punching bag for my ex's whims.

But that was all over now. I would never experience something so horrible again. I got to know what being loved and cared for felt like when I met Jason. He respected me and made me realise that I was worth so much more. It was only because of Jason that I was able to look at the brighter side of the world. He kept pushing me to move forward and cope with the situation in my head. Whenever I felt down, Jason would sit beside me, talk to me and hug me until I felt better.

There were times when I wanted to leave everything and go. I couldn't understand what was happening. I felt like I had no heart and no emotions for anyone in the world, including Jason.

It was Jason who showed me that he cared for me; he made sure that I knew that he wanted me around. He made me see my worth. When my mental health was at its worst, Jason encouraged me and motivated me to go for counselling. He wanted nothing more but for me to get better. I started overthinking everything, which made me more anxious and made my anxiety worse.

My ex-fiancé never supported me with my deteriorating mental health. He thought I was faking it all to get his attention. Yes! I wanted attention. But I wanted his attention of supporting me through life's crises. I wanted his love, and I wanted him to tell me that it would all be okay. But he never did.

It was hard for me to believe that someone could actually care and love one person regardless of the situation. Jason became my rock in those trying times. He paid all the bills, took care of food, and made sure we had a roof over our heads. He did all this even when I was not able to continue my job due to my mental health.

Jason booked an online appointment for me with a therapist. I wanted to go there in person, but I couldn't because of COVID-19. I had an online appointment every week for an hour. The therapist would ask me all about my day, what I did that day and how my life was going. She wanted to know every little detail from me, and it made me feel better somehow. My therapist constantly told me that no one could help my situation other than myself. She told me that only I could find a way to cope with the situation.

My therapist told me that she was there for me whenever I needed someone to talk to. And so, I started relying on and trusting her. I would tell her everything, what I was feeling and how my day went. These sessions went on for a few months.

After months of online therapy, one day, I woke up feeling different. I felt like all the weight had been lifted off my chest. I felt free and genuinely happy. After months, I finally felt like have the power to control my body and my mind. I knew I had moved on, and my ex-fiancé was now just someone from my past who had no control over me.

There still are days when I think about my ex-fiancé and the pain and emotional torture he had given me. But I am happy that it doesn't impact my mind the way it did before. Even today, it makes me feel sad that I was in such a bad condition, but I know how to overcome those thoughts now. To do this, I know how to keep moving forward and not let the past ruin me.

It is hard to find someone ready to stand by your side no matter what. When you find that one person who supports you, loves you, and cares for you, never let them go.

# Chapter 17
# The Updated Dream

As people grow and move on with life, their goals and dreams change. It is part of a person's growth, and it is also essential for them to move forward with their life. I am no different; I had dreams and aspirations as a young girl but growing up brings a change in you. At my present stage, the difference I witnessed was the strong urge to become a full-time mother. I wanted to have a big family and a beautiful home.

Hearing Jason share his thoughts about having a baby stunned me. I really liked him, but the nature of my last breakup had stopped me from keeping any expectations. Then, to top it off, he proposed to me, which was an even bigger surprise. For a while, I thought no one could replace my ex-boyfriend. I had planned the future with him and had stopped seeing a future after him. But being with Jason was something else; my expectations had been revived through him. He was the perfect guy for me, and I couldn't ask for anyone more or less than him. What separated him from my past relationships was his availability and the fact that he was always attentive. He never withdrew his interest from me, was an eager listener, and would equally share his thoughts and feelings with me. I saw him as the type of man who was up to mad ideal standards, and I wanted to grow with him. So, I started to dream of a future with him.

Soon enough, that dream translated to me becoming the ideal family woman. Of course, I wanted to have a comfortable domicile, but I didn't have any extraordinary expectations set for it. I didn't require a huge swimming pool or a lush lawn. I wasn't dreaming of expansive rooms or fancy hallways. For me, having a house is vital; a fancy monument can take the essence of a home away from it.

Usually, people describe their dream home as something quite posh and luxurious. Now, everyone is entitled to their own opinion, but I feel that somewhere along the way, we all began to chase a different ideal. Eventually, home becomes a place to upscale, store an ever-increasing pile of possessions, and pursue a never-realised perfection, the kind portrayed in home catalogs and Instagram pictures.

To me, a home is a place where you feel safe. When you come back after a long day, you feel safe and rested. The world outside seems foreign, something that you can't see yourself spending time in by the end of the day. Unknowingly, you're thankful for this abode that you come back to. You don't care for the architecture; what matters is the comfort and safety it gives you. It offers a place to relax and unwind. It provides an opportunity for interaction among family members—a safe harbor from the storms of life to find acceptance, security, and stability.

And now, along with that beautiful home, I wanted a family, a husband, and children. Jason had already started to fuel this dream by sharing his thoughts about having a baby and asking me to marry him.

I dreamt of my kids becoming teenagers, debating meaningful issues with each other, with Jason, and me. A house that is made on materialistic grounds becomes centered around its possessions. I wanted my family to own their home for the people in it, for the memories they create, not for the fancy aspect of it.

My new dream was making me look into a happy future. The image of the whole family being together on evenings and various other occasions excited me. I wanted that eagerly. I wanted to get pregnant so that Jason and I could have a family.

But the problem was that I didn't see that happening. Since Jason had surprised me with the conversation, we had been trying to get pregnant. But, we were in no luck. Each time I felt I was ovulating, we would try our best to get fertile, but the tests showed no changes. My belly remained flat. I started to think if I was infertile, and my mental health started to get affected again.

I felt various aspects of my life started to get affected by it. My physical, emotional, sexual, and spiritual; all aspects of my life had started to get affected. When I read about it online, I learnt that the most common mental health concerns reported by fertility patients are symptoms of anxiety and depression. So, I discussed it with Jason, and we decided to seek out treatments for it.

I looked into treatments online, and it got me into a further state of worry. I learnt that the more physically and emotionally demanding and intrusive patients' medical treatments become, the higher the reported symptoms of anxiety and depression. Each passing monthly cycle could bring a roller coaster ride of emotions such as anger, betrayal, guilt, sadness, and even hope.

I told Jason about everything that I read online, and he dismissed me, saying that people write whatever they want; it doesn't mean anything. But I am sure that while comforting me, he was hesitating. He tried to conceal his worry as best he could. Of course, I understood well enough that he was going through the same thoughts as I was.

I also read online that infertility can drive away partners from each other. Many couples have sex as a way to connect emotionally. When sex becomes associated with failure and frustration, couples may lose their emotional connection. The pressure to perform or have sex due to infertility treatments can isolate partners and divide couples. As I read it, my mind started to go into overdrive. Jason was a blessing to me, and the connection I had with him was the one I always wanted. He cared for me and was deeply devoted to me, and I didn't want to lose him because of infertility issues.

I didn't even know if one of us was infertile. I just kept reading and researching it since it wasn't happening for me. But I had also read of cases where a couple couldn't get pregnant for a while, and it just happened for them after some time. In my case, the disturbing factor was that I had gotten pregnant so quickly in previous years. At that time, the child was unwanted, but when I actually wanted to be a mother, it wasn't happening for me.

My friends and family said that it was probably my stress coming in the way of my fertility; that didn't seem like a problem to me. The reason for my anxiety was that I wasn't able to get pregnant. But before that, I wasn't stressing about anything. In fact, all the stress prior to that related to my ex-fiancé. And since Jason, all the previous worrying and stressing out had faded away. I was having the best days of my life with Jason until I found out that I couldn't get pregnant.

Having so many dreams and wanting a simple lifestyle had surged hope in me. I could clearly envision a beautiful house with wonderful kids and Jason by my side. And when you're eager to get something, and it doesn't seem to be happening for you, it puts you in a wholly lost state. So, my mind would always be occupied with thoughts of my fertility. Even if I'd engage in a conversation, somehow, I would become lost in my own thoughts.

Soon I was consumed by my depressed state. Jason was also worried about me. But what could even he do? We had been going over our options. However, I was too afraid to visit any fertility facility. I was worried about what I would find out and what the doctors would suggest.

I would just lay down every night and hope I would get pregnant anyhow. Reading about other women also lifted up my hopes. In many cases, those women thought they would be barren for life, but they were expecting a kid one day. I wondered if that would be the case for me. That after a long wait, I would finally be pregnant. But I couldn't wait that long. I couldn't be uncertain about having a kid. It had become my dream, and I wanted it to be fulfilled. The hurt and stress were building up. I hoped for a miracle.

Whenever I saw myself in the mirror and didn't see a bump on my belly, I didn't understand why it was not happening to me. Each day, my train of thoughts would compel the most irrational beliefs to let me feel as if there was something wrong with me. I would admit that my mind did touch thoughts of patience and solution. But, they were always overpowered with the feeling that perhaps my body would never carry a baby. I continually felt something was wrong with me, to a point where it affected my self-image. Life was good, but I held onto only one thing that I did not have.

Each time Jason cuddled me at night, I would think that he may never be able to hold our kids like that. There wasn't much that we could do here. We just needed our bodies to do what they were meant to do. However, I did realise that it's not always possible for our bodies to function optimally. And you cannot really know what the case is for sure if you don't seek medical help. For some people, it never happens; for others, it's a long test of patience. It was surely the wait for us that we decided to give priority over other methods.

# Chapter 18
# Making It Happen

Being able to conceive a child is nothing less than a miracle. And so far, Jason and I were out of luck to expect such a blessing. Things just weren't working out on that front, and we both felt terrible about it. The inability to conceive was making me anxious and depressed. I wanted a child. I desired to hold my baby in my arms.

The most precious jewels a woman could ever wear around her neck are a child's loving arms, and I really wanted to experience that feeling. Unfortunately, my ex had denied my dream for so long that I found it unbearable to wait.

My heart ached whenever I saw another woman cuddling her child. I really wanted to have a soft, little, cuddly baby of my own. I am not a jealous person; I just envy women who are fortunate enough to be mothers. It is my dream to be a mother—a mother who would spoil her child to bits. And yet, raise the child well, such that he or she is a productive and virtuous member of society.

I was willing to sacrifice anything just to have a child. And this time around, my partner Jason was very supportive of my dream. It was his dream too. It's what made my relationship with him so special. Since we both shared this wish, finally, in June/July

2020, Jason and I agreed to get help with getting pregnant. I felt something was not right. Friends and family suggested that I might be stressed and would need to calm down. Somehow, I did not feel this was the case. I didn't understand why I was unable to conceive. The fact that I got pregnant quite quickly the last time left me feeling worried about why I wasn't able to get pregnant again. I just couldn't understand why this was happening to me.

I was at a loss as to why I was unable to conceive. I felt as though there was a void in my heart. I often felt helpless and lost in my circumstances. I badly wanted a child, so much so that I often thought of adoption or surrogacy. But those were options that did not meet my heart's desires. I wanted my own child—my own flesh and blood.

Jason was extremely supportive and caring. He wanted this to work as much as I did, if not more. We both wanted to have a child together. It would not only signify our love for one another but bring a new life into this world. This was our dream of having a family. We wanted a child to add the finishing touches and complete our lives. I understand that raising a child is not a piece of cake, but Jason and I were more than willing to take up this feat.

I didn't want to go on the waiting list for the National Health Service (NHS). I just did not want to wait. So, I searched online for private clinics. One of the clinics stood out as it was rated as one of the best fertility clinics. We are not very well off, but we had savings. So, we decided to use some of our savings for this procedure. We went back and forth. We had to undergo a lot of tests. It turned out that neither of us had any fertility concerns. Yet, something, somewhere, was quite wrong, because of which I could not conceive.

So, the next stage was for me to undergo a procedure called Hysterosalpingocontrast Sonography (HyCoSy). This was a procedure whereby my fallopian tubes would be flushed. Normally, the procedure took place when the patient was conscious, but in my case, I needed to be sedated.

When I awoke, the nurse informed me that I could not get pregnant naturally. A feeling of numbness took over me. I didn't know how to respond. I was in shock, to say the least. Why was my dream becoming so unachievable? All I wanted was a child. I felt inadequate because Jason and I could not be blessed with a child, all because of me. For countless nights, I wondered what Jason thought about this. I always worried that he might resent me because of my inability to conceive.

It killed me inside to think that perhaps I could not bear a child. Not only was I anxious, but I also showed symptoms of depression. My life was at an all-time low. It seemed as though things could only get worse from here.

I was heartbroken to hear the dreadful piece of news. While I did comprehend what the nurse had just told me, I could not process it. The nurse explained that both my fallopian tubes were damaged beyond repair. I believe that the STI (Chlamydia or Gonorrhoea) that I had suffered from for many years was to blame.

My mother was with me at the time, and we went straight back to her place. I was devasted, not being able to think straight. I kept thinking about how I would break the horrible news to Jason. Nothing made any sense to me then. It took a lot of strength and determination to hold myself together and maintain the loving bond that I shared with Jason.

I had been tested for Chlamydia in my teens, after which I received treatment and even got pregnant with my ex. I believe I contracted some infection or disease from him. As soon as I had the abortion in my teens, I went straight on the pill, and I never discontinued it until I started trying for a baby with Jason. When I quit the pill, my body felt different. I had terrible pains in my lower stomach. The pain was very intense. Eventually, I did end up going to A&E to get myself checked. The doctor referred me to my GP for an ultrasound scan. I was scanned, and apparently, everything was normal. My GP carried out the smear, and the results showed the presence of abnormal cells. I had to go to the hospital and have another scan.

Fortunately, the doctor explained it was normal and self-limiting. Yet, my mind was filled with anxious thoughts. I was thinking about everything I had already been through, and I couldn't wrap my head around the results of all the tests. Just thinking about the fact that I could not conceive naturally made me ask myself, "Why me? What have I done to deserve this?" I had wanted a child my whole life, and here I was, being told that I couldn't conceive.

During my teens, I was in love with the show 'Teen Mom.' I enjoyed watching the programme because of the mother-daughter bond that the show portrayed. I desperately wanted such a bond. But I wanted my partner to have the same feelings about having a child together. I wanted him to show me through his actions or else tell me in literal terms that he wished for this miracle too.

Jason is the one. He showed me that there was light at the end of the tunnel. Like myself, he wanted to have a child. It all felt like it was a dream until I found out that I could not conceive naturally.

Sometimes I feel that the devil is watching over me. At times, I think my ex still controls me and ensures that I do not get up to anything he dislikes. But was my ex the reason for my inability to conceive? He was the last person I was with before Jason, and I had been with him for ten whole years! Did he really do this to me?

My ex and I had broken up twice, and he had admitted that he had been sexually active with other girls. How did it make sense that I had to get myself tested for STIs, but he didn't? His excuse was that if I didn't have any disease or infection, he wouldn't either. He never got himself tested, not even once.

Despite everything I have been through, I was not one to give up. My motto is to 'keep fighting.' I wasn't going to give up on my dream that easily. Jason and I were committed to making every effort to have a child.

So, the next stage was to go through another procedure whereby my eggs and Jason's sperm were collected. It seemed to me that Jason had the easiest job. As for me, I had to take medications and inject myself every day up until the day of the procedure, which was 10-11 days away. I could not do it myself, so Jason administered the medicine every evening. I have a very low threshold for pain, and part of my stomach got bruised from it. I remember I used to cry every time I had to go through it.

Jason disliked having to put me through all that pain, but he kept saying, "Do it for our baby." His presence and support throughout this phase and the act of repeating those encouraging words out loud every time kept me going. I never gave up hope. Hope strengthened me and kept me alive despite all the hardships I went through.

With everything that was going on in my life regarding my health, it was unfortunate that I had to leave my job. I found everything overwhelming, and I felt I couldn't cope. Depression gnawed at me. I wouldn't feel happy going to work. I just wanted to be at home. Eventually, I decided that my health came first, so I resigned.

Coming back to the procedure I was undergoing, I had to be sedated for my eggs to be collected. Later, I was told that the results were eleven. I was on top of the world and had the biggest smile on my face. I was pleased because I hadn't expected the results to be eleven. I had expected the worst.

Having heard this news, I felt positive. However, as days went by, depression started to hit me again. Some of the eggs didn't survive the fertilisation stage. Some of them didn't survive the biopsy stage. As per the preceding results, I was told that there were two eggs left. But I wouldn't get the final results to confirm the suspicions until 25 March 2021.

At that stage, I was still hopeful that I would conceive. I was confident that my miracle would come through too.

# Chapter 19
# IVF Treatments

Months passed by, and as the day of the final results slowly started approaching, my anxiety began to increase. A part of me was waiting for the outcome. However, at the same time, I was terrified because what if things went wrong?

How would it affect me if I did not get an opportunity to become a mother, a role I have wanted to play for a long time?

Instead of spending my days worrying, I decided to switch things up for the better. It was not like negative thoughts did not pop up in my mind; they did. But I wanted to focus on positivity. So, even though I was prepared for the worst, I still practiced being a mother. I watched informational shows again, read many books, conversed with various mothers, and acquired every tidbit of information I could find from different sources to help me take care of our baby. Of course, everyone complained about how tough it was, but I was ready for it. I knew I would never complain, especially after the struggle I went through.

I had phone calls from the clinic each day, or let's say every other day. The purpose of the calls was to explain the results of each embryo. Eleven eggs were collected, and tests were a must to be processed to confirm whether each embryo would survive or not. It was heartbreaking. Each day, the amount was getting smaller and smaller. I kept thinking about the worst, not having any left to survive.

However, the results left me speechless. I was told that we had one perfect embryo and one with no results. Jason and I decided to go ahead with the perfect embryo and kept the other embryo stored and frozen for a year. Once again, I had to be sedated and just had to hope for the treatment to be successful. Before the embryo was planned to be inserted, I had to take medications and injections again. It was time to prepare my body to think it was pregnant. The doctor also suggested a womb scratch. It was recommended for the embryo to stick to my cervix, and I went ahead to be sedated for this too. Jason and I had all our hopes for one chance. We only had one embryo, which was perfect. If it didn't work, I personally thought I would have a mental breakdown. Because we would have to go through the whole procedure again, but the money was overwhelming, and we only had one chance due to the cost.

The doctor instructed me to take a pregnancy test seven days after the procedure. The doctor would not know if the procedure worked till after a certain number of days. Those seven days were the heaviest for me because I was desperate to see what my future had in store for me. Was I finally going to become a mother? I kept staring at the clock, waiting for time to pass, and as I marked off each day from my calendar, I felt happy.

I could not wait any longer, so I decided to take two pregnancy tests on the 6th day. As soon as the day arrived, I woke up early in the morning and took it. The other one I took at my father's. When I took the test at his place, I got the desired result. I told Jason about it, and he was pleased. However, he did not want to get my hopes up again, so he explained that it might not be true because of the medicines that could have triggered it. Deep inside my heart, I also knew that.

By now, I had become increasingly impatient and wanted to know the answer right away. My appointment was the next day, and it felt like a lifetime of waiting.

This was the reason why I had to stay at my father's the night before, as Jason was unable to come because of work. He always took time off from work to take me to the clinic in the past, so I did not blame him for not being there.

As I lay in bed that night, all sorts of mixed thoughts clouded my mind. There were positive ones, where I imagined myself holding the most precious baby in my arms and a happy family picture being taken. Then there were also negative ones where I imagined myself crying and blaming myself for being unlucky. Because of all this, it was hard for me to doze off to sleep that night.

When the next day arrived, I got up and dressed myself. My father was outside waiting for me in his van. It felt like I was on a rollercoaster ride. One minute I would feel excited, and the next minute, I would feel nervous and hopeless. This continued to happen the entire way there.

Finally, after stepping into the clinic, I mustered up all my strength and informed the receptionist that I had arrived. I was directed to the waiting area, where I sat down looking at all the other women who had the same expressions as mine. We were all in the same boat, desperately seeking an answer to eliminate all our worries. As the time kept ticking, I waited for my name to be called. I started quivering with fear because I had no idea what would happen in the next few minutes.

Finally, my name was called, and I heaved a sigh of relief. I went up to the receptionist and asked where I was supposed to go. She stated a room upstairs, and I knew that was my destination for the day. I had no idea what my emotions would be like after coming out of it.

As I started walking towards the room, I took deep breaths. So many questions were coming to my mind. *What would happen if the embryo did not work? What would happen if it did, but something else went wrong?*

I could not help myself. These negative thoughts had become a part of me now due to everything I had faced in the past. I always felt so conflicted because of my thoughts.

When I reached the room, I greeted the sonographer standing near the screen. There was a small bed there, so I quietly lay down. The only thing that was audible in the room was the sound of my heart racing rapidly. I refrained from looking at the screen as much as possible due to the pressure of thinking that I might not have my baby inside me.

*"Congratulations! You're pregnant,"* I heard a voice that echoed in the room, and my body felt numb.

*"WHAT? I AM PREGNANT?"* I could not believe what I had just heard. How was this even happening?

*"Yes, you are. I am so happy for you!"* the sonographer said as she showed me the screen, and I saw the baby's heart flickering on it. Uncontrollable tears fell from my eyes to my cheeks, feeling relieved. I was more than delighted, and I thought about Jason. How would he feel about this whole situation? After struggling for so long, I knew I deserved this. Happiness was finally knocking at my door.

Every person in the world deserves a happy ending. I hoped all the other women sitting in the waiting room would receive great news, too. I reminisced on my teen self and pondered upon how I wanted to get married, be loved, finally have a family of my own, and live happily ever after. Of course, I had other goals I wanted to accomplish, but I could not sideline this one.

My baby's due date was 27th January 2022, and our journey of becoming parents was near. All the emotions I felt, heartaches, sadness, tearfulness, joy, and hope, seemed to make sense to me now. I would be able to appreciate my baby even more.

There was a sudden flashback of all the previous months and how far I had come in my journey. My mental health had taken a toll, and I was struggling. It was hard enough to move on from my ex-fiancé, and now I had to go through IVF. It made my blood boil thinking that he was the sole cause behind my condition. I knew I needed professional help, so I began counselling sessions soon after my ex was no longer in my life.

Unfortunately, the torture still lingered in my mind, and I felt like he was still around to control my life. I quickly controlled my thoughts and began focusing on IVF. It helped me to forget about my ex for some time. However, he will always be a part of me, even though I had learnt to deal with situations that revolved around him.

I recalled how I was given dates of the procedures for the embryo to be inserted. Different dates had been provided to me throughout the month. And different medications were given to me to initiate the treatment for my body to prepare. At that time, I was working, and every day seemed difficult, mentally and physically.

The worst part was that the clinic was not down the road.

It was based in Central London, and to travel there and back to work left me exhausted. I wanted to focus on my health before I lost it completely. Due to these circumstances, I had to hand in my notice. I could not cope with work due to personal reasons. We had only one chance at a single perfect embryo, and I did not want to lose it because of my stress. Jason and I had put in a lot of money to go through this and to make our dreams come true. He had been the most supportive person. We needed money to spend a good life, but Jason also knew how essential it was to hope for a healthy baby. He saw me crying every day, losing my mind, but still, he never left my side.

My anxiety and depression affected me badly. I felt my body and mind could not cope with life. It felt things were coming one after another. And I really would not know how I would cope if something did not work. It also makes life harder when you see other people living your dream, and you think you want it more than them, but it doesn't happen for you. Then, you are only left wondering, '*why did this happen to me?*'

I've never asked for much, just a normal fairytale ending. But every life has its devils to ruin parts of your life or make you fight for what you want in life. I know there are others out there in the world who are going through a difficult situation or fighting for their dream. But at the same time, I am the person who is going through this life. No one else can help you unless you get the help you need or help yourself. No matter what the circumstances are. We are all dealing with a problem or fear. It knows how to control yourself in the right shape and form. Sometimes it is harder for some people, and some don't have it as hard as you.

When I found out I was pregnant, I knew this was not the end. Anything could still happen throughout the pregnancy. I decided to finish counselling as I needed to focus on my pregnancy. It was the right moment to do so. I did not want to get myself in a state or make myself worse. I wanted to try and take it one day at a time.

# Chapter 20
# All Worth It

What do you do when you are going through a difficult situation? I feel affirmative that the question of *'Why me?'* pops up in your mind now and then when some affliction heads your way. However, that's completely normal, and I do not blame you. When going through a rough situation, we only see the problem before our eyes, but we never focus on the outcome. We are too distracted, disturbed, and depressed because of everything happening in our lives. But then, when we get the result of our patience, we feel a wave of happiness, gratefulness, and satisfaction. Hence, in the end, everything is worth it.

As I glance at the calendar, I notice today's date, which is 18$^{th}$ February 2022. *'Oh, how time flies...'* I think to myself. I went through the hardest time of my life just a while back, and now I have gotten back to my usual self after enduring all the pain. I am currently sitting in front of the computer and writing this chapter, trying to put my heart and soul into it. Picking the right words to express my feelings and being afraid that my baby might wake up at the same time seems like a challenging exercise for the mind. But, hopefully, one day, my child will read this book and become aware of all the struggles I had to face during my entire life. I will feel like a proud mother that day, and the feeling will be unmatchable.

To be honest, I would not say time passed quickly because these painful nine months were hard enough like they are for every woman out there. There are a total of 273 days or 39 weeks in nine months. Every single one of those days, you experience a different emotion. I feel like women should receive a massive round of applause for going through this whole process with immense strength. You never know the true feeling until you have actually gone through it. They say a person cannot truly understand what is happening in your life until they put themselves in your shoes, and I could not agree more.

Pregnancy is hectic, and it brings many changes in your life. The first few trimesters are somewhat bearable, but the real struggle begins with the third one. The third trimester of pregnancy is the last period of pregnancy. New discomforts pave in along with the ones from the second trimester. For example, you may have difficulty breathing and need to urinate more frequently as the baby grows, putting greater strain on your internal organs. This is normal, and these issues should subside once you give birth. You need to have a high amount of patience when you are pregnant because you have to take care of yourself and the little body developing inside of you.

It was the ninth month of my pregnancy, and the due date of the induction was 27th January 2022. The day I would hold the love of my life in my hands was near; it was hard to believe. The feeling was surreal, and I was looking forward to seeing if my baby's face would be identical to his mummy or daddy's.

Soon, we got to know that we were being blessed with a baby boy. I had no personal preference. I knew I would love and take care of my baby regardless of gender, and Jason felt the same. An angel was finally coming to complete our family. We just could not wait to have a little darling walking around our home with his tiny steps.

However, my journey was quite not over. I did not have an easy pregnancy like other lucky women. So, let's start from the very start of the big day that changed our lives forever. When I woke up on the morning of my induction, I first picked my phone up and called the receptionist, excited to know what time I should reach the hospital.

But that's when we received the first piece of bad news of the day. The receptionist told me that there were no available beds for me to be induced. Hearing that definitely formed a worrisome expression on my face. But it was not the end of the world. I knew I would get another bed soon because I was next on the list. I stared at the clock in front of me, waiting for the minutes to tick by quickly. Unfortunately, my anxiety had reached another level by then.

It was not because I was not important to the hospital or that no one cared about my pregnancy. It was only because there were no beds available, but I knew I would be called once they were free. I wanted the bed to be available soon because I was struggling with the heavy weight that was not allowing me to walk properly. It was also because of my arthritis. To put my anxiety on pause mode, I decided to take a nap on the sofa in the living room. However, I put my phone really close to me so as to not miss the bell when it rang. It was essential to be cautious, so I did not miss out on my turn.

Finally, my phone started ringing, waking me up from my nap. The pain persisted; in fact, it had grown even more potent. The person on the other end of the phone told me that a bed was available and I could come in.

After hearing those words, my happiness reached to another level. I just wanted my baby to come into this world with mummy and daddy because it would be the safest place. I broke the news out to Jason, and he seemed delighted. He was just as excited as I was. He quickly took the keys and went outside with me. During this whole process, he never made me feel alone, not even for a single second. I guess that is what we truly seek in a partner. Most people will be there for you in your good times, but they will come up with lame excuses when you need them. I carefully sat down in the car, trying my best to struggle with the extra weight of my baby.

I'll be honest. The whole car ride was a rollercoaster of emotions because my feelings were continuously transitioning.

First, I felt happy. But two minutes later, that happiness turned into fear. But that was understandable, right? When you go through so much in life and happiness knocks at your door, you feel a little sceptical. It takes you some time to process the reality because you are so used to struggling. Will my pregnancy proceed successfully? I had no idea. However, I knew that whatever happened, it would be for the better.

When we reached the hospital, Jason got out of the car. He supported me while I struggled to walk when entering the building. We arrived at the ward, and I was taken to my bed by a couple of hospital staff members, who were lovely enough to greatly help me. It was not very comfortable, to say the least, but it was enough. I just had to get done with the process as soon as possible because I could not wait to hold my baby in my arms.

A machine was put around my stomach for monitoring purposes, and I had to wait for about an hour. A midwife in the room was taking so much care of me. She asked if I was feeling any contractions. However, at that time, I was not, so I simply said no. The midwife glanced at the monitor, and she said I had them according to the graph displayed on the monitor. She said I needed to go to another room where induction took place and planned to break my water. Let me tell you, that was purely a nightmare for me.

During pregnancy, your baby is enclosed by the amniotic fluid in the amniotic sac, which cushions and protects your newborn baby. Amniotic fluid also assists in the development of your baby's lungs and digestive system while maintaining a constant temperature in the environment. Your baby's urine makes up the majority of the fluid during the second half of pregnancy, but nutrients, hormones, and antibodies (which help fight infection) are also present. The sac membranes break before the commencement of labor, later during delivery, or even before labor begins in certain circumstances. This is referred to as 'water breaking.' It's one of the first indicators of labor, yet medical professionals aren't sure why your water breaks.

The midwife will try and poke your water with something that looks like a crochet hook to break it. You may experience (very minor) discomfort as the device enters your vagina, but most women only experience a large, warm gush of liquid when their water breaks. My midwife advised me to tell her if I felt lightheaded. The overall process was excruciating. To help me be more relaxed, the midwife gave me some Entonox, or should I say in simpler words, laughing gas. The more deep breaths I took, the more I started to feel lightheaded than I was before. Finally, I was conscious enough to hear mixed voices around me. I pushed myself and finally came back to reality. Even after going through so much pain, knowing that my water didn't break shattered my heart.

They all persuaded me to rest and try again. However, even the second time did not work. The midwife suggested I go into the labor ward for consultation instead. She told me that if it still did not work, I should try a medicine called 'Cytotec.' When going into the labor ward, they knew I would need support, so they called Jason to come and stand by my side during the procedure. After another painful attempt, it still did not work. At that point, I could not describe my feelings. It was an actual moment of despair.

The day had just started, and it had already felt so long. The only thing I wanted to do now was to push my baby out and take it home. When I went back to the induction room, I was in immense pain, and tears began to shed from my eyes. It was because of the contractions that had begun to kick in. About two hours later, the midwife checked again. She told me that the medicine was not working, and the contractions had worsened.

After being looked after for quite a couple of hours, the pain diminished. The midwife advised me to rest for the whole day. The following day, I was taken to the labor ward, and I did not know what would happen. However, I did not want to delay this any longer. The midwife told me to take a quick shower to feel better while waiting for Jason to arrive. He went with me again to the labor ward, where we saw another consultant. He said that he would try to break the water again. He hoped the medication I took had worked and had softened my cervix.

Now, the pain was more intense than before, and I felt tired of using gas and air to help me feel more relaxed. It was really difficult because they kept asking me to relax for the water to break, which I could not do so easily. It was my first ever pregnancy, so it was obviously hectic. After trying for the fourth time, the water finally broke, and I could not feel more relieved. Usually, what doctors do is if your water hasn't burst, the doctor, midwife, or nurse will attempt to break it before you become fully dilated. This allows them to figure out whether you have any issues preventing the baby from being delivered safely. After your water breaks, your contractions will typically become much more intense, and labor moves considerably quickly.

Since my water had broken now, I was dilated about two to three centimeters after waiting for many hours. The doctors wanted the process to speed up, so they suggested that I put on a drip to help and offered me to get an epidural, which is an injection in your back to stop you from feeling pain in any part of your body. I was really against it, though. I never planned to take so many medicines and wanted a quick and simple pregnancy. However, fate had different plans for me. I wanted my child's birth to be done naturally, but things were not going according to my plan. So I finally gave in, and I cannot emphasise how tired I felt.

I honestly have no idea how I kept going. I held on to Jason tightly because he was my only support at that time. I asked him to keep me still because the process took longer than I had imagined. I had never felt this type of pain before.

Jason played a huge role in my pregnancy because he took care of me and our cat, who was at home. Her name is Tia, and we were constantly worried if she was fine. We considered her a part of our family; it was our responsibility to take care of her. It did not bother me if Jason was going home because I felt like I was getting better. He did it for our sake. We both knew I was nowhere near to pushing our baby out.

After a long wait of 23 hours, almost an entire day, the doctors and a midwife came into the room. I was resting and was ready to discuss the next stage. The doctor said that the process of dilation was still going on. However, he was concerned about an infection that could have potentially formed in my bladder. And so, I had to get an emergency C-section, and words cannot describe how scared I was.

First, they gave me another epidural to ease the pain a little bit. I had to relax my shoulders and bend my back in a certain way. Then, they used a certain cold spray to check if I was numb from my stomach to my legs. After taking all the precautionary steps, they covered me with a blue sheet, and Jason was standing right next to me. I felt pleased to see him, and throughout the procedure, I kept looking at him. He seemed to calm me down perfectly, and I was clueless about what I would have done if it were not for him. I insisted that he keep talking to me because it was the perfect distraction.

Just a few minutes later, I heard the cries of our baby. It was the most beautiful sound I had ever heard. Jason let out a small squeal because he was more than excited. Our family was finally going to be completed, and everything that happened was truly worth the wait. Jason went over to cut our baby's cord, and I watched as much as I could see. It was such a happy and memorable moment for our family. Seeing your child for the first time ignites a strong feeling of being overwhelmed with emotion, as if you're so packed with love that you're about to burst. As you gaze at this small miracle, you are overwhelmed with amazement and wonder.

I heard voices echoing in the whole room, and everyone kept coming to admire our baby. The midwife weighed him and wrapped him up. He weighed 9 pounds and 5oz. I did not have enough strength to hold him, but I kept staring at him. I was shifted to another ward after the procedure, and this time, Jason was holding him. Jason becoming a daddy was a dream come true for me. I finally had a family now, and even though it was the end of my pregnancy, a new beginning started for me.

Jason came closer to me, and we mutually decided on a name for him. His innocent face and soft smile were completely enchanting, and we thought the name 'Daniel' would be perfect for our little angel. This was the name that we both chose while I was pregnant.

I was told I had lost 700 milliliters of blood and was given medication and injections to prevent blood clots and infections. I finally held Daniel in my arms, and he did not cry. He seemed so relaxed and content. I felt the happiest knowing that he was mine.

No one said pregnancy was easy, but after toiling through all the procedures and medications, the miracle that comes out of your body makes it all seem worth it. I finally have someone I can give all my love to, make a perfect little world for, and protect from everything wrong in the world. The time for me to become a mother and take care of my baby finally arrived. This is all I ever wanted to complete my life. A beautiful miracle has come true. Now, we can start raising our home, our perfect lives, and our own little family.

Printed in Great Britain
by Amazon

45196806R00106